I'M MOVING
TWO

968-SERD

I'M MOVING
TWO

*A Poetic Journey
with Dystonia*

Beka Serdans, RN

8-SERD

To order additional copies of this book, contact:
Xlibris Corporation
1-888-7-XLIBRIS
www.Xlibris.com
Orders@Xlibris.com

DEDICATED TO MY FATHER, IMANTS SERDANS AND MY GRANDPARENTS.

ACKNOWLEDGMENTS :

Special thanks for supporting the first chapbook (Dystonia is...A Personal Perspective, 1998) endeavor of this poetic journey :
The Dystonia Medical Research Foundation
Chicago, Illinois

A very special thanks to Dr. Mitchell F. Brin, M.D.; Director of the Movement Disorders Program at Mount Sinai Medical Center, N.Y., NY USA ; for being the first to recognize the value of this writing project for other patients.

A "second" special thanks to my three "best friends" :
M.J.M., L.R.S., A.F.
for always "being there", supporting me wholeheartedly and encouraging me to establish Care 4 Dystonia; an organization dedicated to creating support services for people with dystonia.

Much of this book could not have been written if I had never had the opportunity to work with colleagues in the Critical Care Division at Columbia Presbyterian Medical Center in New York City. Their kind and unselfish support in times of need have been much appreciated and will not be forgotten. I feel privileged and honored to continue to be able to work with all of them. Space limits my mentioning every person by name but you all are "very special" to me even more so as the effects of dystonia become more visible. The ICU Staff at Highland Hospital in Rochester, New York deserve special recognition as they have guided my nursing career during times of success and disappointment. They have seen the "best and worst of me" over the years, always being tolerant and giving.

Heartfelt Thanks to All Always- Beka

DYSTONIA IS . . .

Something's wrong with my neck.
I'm the only one who knows this.
No one else knows.
There's a pulling sensation.
A drifting to the left.
I wonder what I did ?
Constant stiffness.
May be it's all the heavy wine I brought back from Europe ?
I really should stop carrying those heavy suitcases.
But I never seem to learn.

Dystonia . . .

My neck isn't any better.
Its been unmovable for three days.
Bought an electric heating blanket.
I hope it will help.
Heat is supposed to help spasms.
Of any form.

Dystonia is . . .

The neck stiffness is unbearable.
I have never experienced anything like this.
I'll try some Advil.
Driving is nearly impossible.
I begin to rely on the public transit system.

Dystonia is . . .

Sent myself to the physician's office.
Who says very little.
Other than "it's a strained muscle" -a strained neck muscle.
From what ?
Try some heat and Advil.
I do and have already done so for the last few days.
I suppose I'll follow his advice.
He's got the M.D. initials behind his name.
I'm simply an R.N.
An Intensive Care Unit Registered Nurse.
An intelligent one.
And I don't believe his diagnosis.

Dystonia is . . .

I've stayed in bed for 2 days.
Things have improved.
I haven't burned the house down with the electric blanket yet.
The wine has been extremely helpful.
The physician's advice hasn't.

Dystonia is . . .

A week has gone by.
I now have complete mobility of my head and neck.
I hope the neck stiffness never returns.
I'm ready to tackle the Intensive Care Unit again.
Life is back to normal.

Dystonia is . . .

I've been sick with the stomach bug.
Worn-out leaves fall to the ground.

A hint of winter air is upon us.
My doctor gives me an antibiotic for a so-called "stomach bug".
I think he's missing something.
From a diagnostic point of view.
I've had this stomach bug for a couple of months now.
Should we blame it on the European wine ?
There is something that's not right here.
The neck strain is back again.
My doctor is probably tired of hearing about my complaints.
I've been told that "I'm stressed".

> "I'm like this because I want to go to medical
> school".
> "I'm a female."
> "I'm demented and depressed".

OK ,what if I am all these things ?
But.

I'm not.
I can't imagine ever saying such things to a patient.
It's not good medicine.
It's a disgrace.
And I'm embarrassed that I work with such people.

Dystonia is . . .

More physical complaints have developed.
Over a course of a few months.
Am I disillusioned ?
But they're valid complaints to me.
Validity.
Something we all need at certain points in our lives.

Dystonia is . . .

Today I find myself in the local Emergency Department as a
patient.
I cannot walk straight.
I tilt to the left.
My mind is preoccupied with my left side.
What happened to my right side ?
That's my dominant side.
It is a funny sensation.
They called in the same neurologist who told my father that his
paraplegia was a side-effect of chemotherapy.
My father had a spinal tumor.
A four minute neurological exam.
They can see that I can't walk straight.
But they're sending me home anyway.
The person next to me has a headache.
He's getting a spinal tap.
What am I getting ?
An unnecessary medical bill.
They say my symptoms are due to the antibiotic.
The antibiotic that is supposed to rid me of this on-going "stomach
bug".
In ten years of nursing I have never heard of this side-effect.
My colleagues question the medical decisions-made today.
They are all RN's.
We always question everything.
It's called being a informed healthcare consumer.

I sign the discharge sheet and head for home.
I leave believing that my doctor thinks I'm psychotic.
It's true.

But the eyes can be very revealing.
I leave leaning to the left.

BEKA SERDANS, RN

On the arms of my friend.
As people watch.

And say nothing.

Dystonia is . . .

Two days have passed.
I'm still leaning to the left.
My mother is worried.
But then mothers never stop worrying.
No matter how old you are.

Dystonia is . . .

I saw the neurologist today.
He's baffled.
So am I.

Dystonia is . . .

The pulling neck sensation is back again.
Only I can tell that it's there.
No one else knows.
But me.

Dystonia is . . .

I seek information.
About me and these unusual symptoms.
That no one seems to believe.
I enter the big local medical library .
I love the stacks there.
Despite dust and all.

I'M MOVING TWO

Filtering pages
Countless books and journals.

So many writers.
Whose contributions remain unknown to others.
I could easily reside in the stacks.
Leaving reality behind me.
They say that knowledge is powerful medicine.

I agree.
But it seems that the more you know, the more likely it is for
others to feel threatened by your questions and actions.
I'm sure that I've intimidated every physician I've seen so far.
And I've seen a lot !
About five so far.
I sifted through several chapters about neck disorders.
And finally I found a description of my symptoms.
Including a picture.
They call it SPASMODIC TORTICOLLIS.
An unusual name for a rare disorder.
How did I get this ?
Why couldn't my physician find this in his neurology textbook ?

Dystonia is . . .

I'm finding that I can't keep my hands away from my face and neck.
My mentor who happens to be a successful surgeon yelled at me.
He said I would never get through a medical school interview with
my hands in my hair.
I know this.
What am I supposed to do ?
It's an automatic thing.
I'm not trying to be a fashion model.

Dystonia is . . .

Pushing beds in the Recovery Room is becoming unbearable.
The left side of the hallway now has many dent marks.
I confess — it's my fault.
I jokingly tell my patients "I'm a bad driver".
I can't steer.
To the right.
Since my head keeps drifting to the left.
And I don't know how to stop it from doing so.
Without using my hands.

Dystonia is . . .

I returned to the neurologist today.
And tell him I had SPASMODIC TORTICOLLIS.
He laughs.
As I leave the office upset.
And close to tears.
Recognizing that I'm right.
With the diagnosis.
The parking lot echoes with laughter.
As I unlock my Nissan.

The hands going up to the neck is a sensory trick.
There's a fancy french name for it.
They call it : geste antagonistique.

Dystonia is . . .

How many other people with this problem have been told that "
it's in your head " ?
What am I going to do ?
Is anyone listening ?

No one understands.
Neither do I.

Dystonia is . . .

Driving is torturous.
I haven't hit anybody on the road yet.
My sister is afraid to climb into the car with me.
I don't think that I'm that bad a driver.
I've arranged all the mirrors, so I don't have to turn at all.
Aren't I clever ?

Dystonia is . . .

I wake up with PAIN.
Sizzling pain.
Sizzling neck pain.
Imagine throwing a bag of raw uncooked peas on a hot pan.
All one hears is sizzling.
That is what my neck feels like.
What did I ever do to deserve this ?
Is the sizzling going to spread ?

Dystonia is . . .

The Advil doesn't help.
The heating blanket doesn't help.
Hot showers don't help.
My water bill is enormous.
Relaxation doesn't either.
Nothing helps.

Except prayer.
This always helps.
In one way or another.

BEKA SERDANS, RN

Dystonia is . . .

UNRELENTLESS.
UNFORGIVING.

Dystonia is . . .

Another visit to the neurologist again.
Is he going to laugh again ?
I don't find any of this amusing.
He finally agrees that I may have TORTICOLLIS.
Finally a diagnosis from an M.D.
Not an R.N.
I ask him some questions about dystonia.
I make him nervous.
I'm simply being a patient.
An informed patient should always ask questions.
He prescribes an anti-cholinergic drug as well as physical therapy.
I hope these therapies work.

Dystonia is . . .

I'm heading off to Aruba.
To the sun and heat.
May be rest will do me some good ?
Wishful thinking . . .

Aruba is paradise.

The sun and sand burn.
I turn into a dark-colored woman.
I meet plenty of people with straight necks.
I started the new drug.
It's called Artane.

I'M MOVING TWO

No beneficial effect felt yet.
As I crawl up a 250 step carved-hill with one hand by my side.
The other wrapped around my neck.
I wonder who did better- me or the senior citizens ?

Dystonia is . . .
Not a psychological disease.
Not a disease caused by stress.
Not a muscle disease.
Not a seizure disorder.
What is it then ?

Dystonia is . . .

Is a MOVEMENT DISORDER.
I've been reading about movement disorders.
It's all rather interesting.
And I've concluded the following:
Dystonia appears to be difficult to treat.
I can't comprehend why people view it as a " hysterical" disease.
Why are physicians so willing to classify every physical symptom as
psychiatric one ?
What does a psychiatric illness have to do with DYSTONIA, a
disorder involving the basal ganglia ?
The control center for movement in your brain.

Dystonia is . . .

It's not a simple diagnosis.
Too much work involved for many physicians.
That many wish to avoid.

Yet the patient suffers.
Over an extended period of time.

Dystonia is . . .

I begin attending physical therapy sessions.
Three times a week.
Apparently, my entire spine is crooked.
Due to the effects of dystonia.
The ultrasound seems to work.
Temporarily.
I'm put in a device called "the traction collar".
It's supposed to straighten me out.
I generally end up hanging from the ceiling for an hour.
Mid-evil device of the 14 Th Century.
Another time period recognized in textbooks only.

Dystonia is . . .

Pasting DO NOT ENTER signs on your car.
In fear that someone will rearrange your rear-view mirrors.
Barring you from driving.

Dystonia is . . .

Things are not improving with this new drug.
Things are not improving with physical therapy.
I'm forgetting things.
It takes me 40 minutes to calculate the dose of an intravenous
blood pressure medication the other day in the ICU.
This is not me.
This is not safe.
I'm forgetful.
Could it be a sign of early Alzheimer's disease ?
Or is it the medication ?

I'd like to know what's happening to me ?

Dystonia is . . .

Is a complex neurological disorder that requires treatment and lifestyle changes.

How true this is.
New strides have been made regarding the management of dystonia.

I'm unaware of them.
What are they ?

Dystonia is . . .

Involves Factors of Inheritance.
Genetics and pedigree trees.
Factors that are fairly strong in dystonia.
A person with a family history of a movement disorder is more likely to develop a form of dystonia than someone who has no family history.
No one in my family has dystonia.
Except ME.

Dystonia is . . .

Finally having an excuse for not mowing the lawn.
Cleaning the house.
Taking out the garbage.
And doing a number of other things.
That involve movement.

Dystonia is . . .

I'm in a bad mood today.
I don't want to act nice to anyone.
Not to my patients.
Not to my colleagues.
Not to the new in-coming residents who desperately need guid-
ance.
As they enter critical-care medicine.
My neck is sizzling.
I need help.
My one patient weighs over 300 pounds.
Picking up an arm for a blood pressure check is hard enough today.
I want to quit.
Things hurt.
My colleagues are unaware of this.
I want to scream.

Dystonia is . . .

No.
No, I don't end up screaming
I grin and bear it all.
Like a bear fishing for salmon on the Colorado River.
I carry on with things despite dystonia.
I question WHY ?
I wonder how long I can keep working like this ?
I haven't met anybody else with dystonia.
Where are they ?
In the US there are over 350,000 people with dystonia.
I'm one of them.

Dystonia is . . .

I've decided to go out on medical disability.
Things have become quite intolerable.
My head has shifted to the left.

Pain is an ever constant problem.
And pushing 200 pound people who are in bed is exhausting work.
Constant twisting and turning.
Even eating is becoming a problem.
This is an experience I never thought I would have to face.
Life certainly has its ups and downs.
This is definitely a downer.

Dystonia is . . .

I'm sent to the local Movement Disorders Clinic.
Will one find Hope there ?
Met the Attending and the Fellow.
One speaks English .
The other one mumbles.
One is tall.
The other is short.
They report that " I have two big muscles involved."
Both on the right side.
How do they know this ?
Is this good or bad ?
How about a prognosis ?

I hear one word "botulinum toxin" muttered.
What is this ?
I sign the consent form for injections involving the use of a poison.
Everything begins to happen too quickly.
Things become a blur.
They begin poking me with needles.
50 units of botulinum toxin.
Are injected.
What incredible pain.
I hope they knew what they were doing.
I thought I was going to die.
I hope this therapy works.

Research time.

Dystonia is . . .

I leave the office stunned.
Not quite comprehending what transpired.
In a matter of minutes.
I walk in silence.
No laughter.
In the Parking lot this time.

Dystonia is . . .

I'm sick.
It's another case of the flu.
Nausea, shakes.
And the chills.
My mother says "I look white".
What is wrong with me ?
The neck is still stiff.
Will it improve ?
Ever ?

Dystonia is . . .

It's Thanksgiving and I'm now 30.
Attend a local dystonia support group.
Members are all older than I- in their 40's and 60's
Retirement age.
Where do I fit in ?
I feel out of place.
They begin to complain about not being able to do the housework.
I complain about not being able to work as a nurse.
I miss my job.
But no one hears me.

I leave .
Will I return ?
Time will tell.
As talk of Palm Springs and retirement continues.

Dystonia is . . .

Christmas.
Spent six hours in the Emergency Department.
They call it dehydration.
An elderly man is delirious.
A six year old is running around.
Looking for play items.
A woman is vomiting across the hallway.
And Kris Kringle is on the radio.
I'm in the hallway waiting to be re-hydrated with intravenous
fluids.
I leave quickly hoping I won't pass out.
I celebrate the holiday.
I question whether the toxin is working.
And whether I'm feeling side-effects from the toxin ?

Dystonia is . . .

I revisit my ICU today.
My colleagues were all glad to see me.
They're all wondering when I'm coming back.
I miss our nightly pizza and Chinese food take-out meals.
No more yoga sessions in the nurse's station.
What must our patients think ?
All want to hear about the "toxin".
The poison that works for dystonia.

Dystonia is . . .

My mentor is retiring.
I spend the last day with him in the Operating Room.
No more last minute drills on the Cardiovascular system.
No more X-ray interpretations.
No more lectures.
I pace throughout the entire surgical procedure.
The twisting and turning never ceases.
Nor does the questioning.

I met my mentor in the ICU.
As all scrambled into patient rooms.
Leaving me behind.
Standing in the middle of the nurse's station alone.
As he walks in looking for his patients at 10 PM.
I introduce myself and immediately like him.
He has a reputation of being highly skilled but rough at the edges.
I ask him if I can spend time observing him in the Operating Room.
Reply received is "yes".
And so, a friendship and mentor-ship is formed.
Lasting for several years.
And beyond.
Into retirement on the sea coast of Cape Cod.

Dystonia is . . .

A sea of black businessman's suits encapsulates me.
I'm crushed between men and computers.
It's the 6 am businessman's flight.
I'm heading out to meet the famous dystonia neurologist.
What am I getting myself into ?
Into New York.
Into Central Park.
The local attending and fellow could not agree on my treatment plan.

There was confusion.
A sense of loss.
I was caught in the middle.
It shouldn't be so.
For anyone.

Dystonia is . . .

Met the famous neurologist.
He reminding me of a leprechaun.
He's intelligent.
Compassionate.
And not arrogant.
This I hope.

He listens.
But isn't this all I have ever asked for from physicians ?
This is all that all patients ask for during appointments.
To be listened to.
To be heard.
Unfortunately, active listening is not taught in medical school.
I suspect he likes to problem-solve.
A definite thinker.
Will he be able to shed some light on my problems ?
I don't want to be too hopeful.

I've met the Dystonia expert.
Certainly an expert.

A 40 minute neurological exam.
I sense competence.
He wants to make an impact in the field of dystonia.
He already has.
Does he know this ?
I've read his scientific articles.

All of them.
I leave the office somewhat relieved.

A definite diagnosis of dystonia, dysphonia, and torticollis.
What a combination !

The traffic is heavy.
75 more blocks to walk.
There's relief and hope.
I can live with this.
With dystonia.
Finally a diagnosis.

Dystonia is . . .

Sirens and a ticket today.
Got caught by the police today.
I was driving from point A to point B.
60 miles in a 35 mile limit zone.
No excuses.
I was asked about my neck.
I told him it was whiplash.
How do you explain dystonia in layman's terms ?
It is not easy.
He wouldn't listen.
He gave me a ticket anyway.

Dystonia is . . .

What is Dysphonia ?
I have it.
My voice has it.

Voice strain.
Breathy speech.

Now I know why I could never be heard.
It's dystonia that affects the vocal cords.
Two types exist.
Me having one form.
Who knows if one form is better than the other ?

Dystonia is . . .

I've returned to work on a part-time basis.
Beka's back.
Work proves to be more difficult than I thought it would be.
I trip over electrical cords and IV poles.
I've become a "klutz".
I run into glass doors.
And trip over my own feet.
Is it my shoes ?
Or is this what dystonia does to people ?

Dystonia is . . .

I'm tired.
I'm tired of living with this disease.
I'm tired of dealing with this on a daily basis.
There's no escape.

Dystonia is . . .

Loss.
There is no loss like one's own loss.
No grief like one's own grief.
There is no dystonia like one's own dystonia.
Learning to cope is a long-drawn out process.

BEKA SERDANS, RN

Full of ups and downs.
This I know.

Dystonia is . . .

I've applied to medical school.
Only one school.
Am I foolish ?
The dystonia has been tolerable.

Thus, the basis for my decision.
I think I would be an reasonable candidate.
I have all of the qualifications.
Grades, MCATs and all.
I feel confident.
It would be a dream come true.
I think I can do it.
It's only four years.
Four years with dystonia.

I've been wishing.
For things to be the way they were before dystonia came along.
Strangers ask me "what it's like ?"
Often I have no reply.

At times I can't remember what it was like to be "normal".
What is "normal" ?
What would I do if my neck and body were straight ?
And not twist and turn.
Savor the moment ? Maybe.
Live LIFE ? YES.
Always.

I've learned.
Simple wishing doesn't change the course or direction of dystonia.

But you do learn to change your daily living patterns.

Dystonia is . . .

My patients are asking me "how I do it ?"
Do what ?
LIVE ??
Work with dystonia ?
I don't know.
I amaze myself.
I amaze everyone.
I chuckle and smile.

Dystonia is . . .

A fixed head and neck posture.
No movement.
Sizzling pain.
Stiffness and clumsiness.
Spasms.
Hoarseness.
Leg twitching.
Unexpected dystonia progression.
Was medical school a wise decision ?

Dystonia is . . .

A recent survey said that torticollis predominates in women.
I wonder why ?
Are we that different ?
We're all human beings.
Regardless of dystonia.

Dystonia is . . .

Another famous neurologist visit.
I'm getting used to waiting.
Waiting for a cure.
The waiting room is full.
Everyone's sitting.
Avoiding eye contact with one another.
Counting the ceiling tiles.
There's 17 of them.
Is it fear ?
Where is the curiosity ?
I want to talk with my fellow counterparts.
We silently watch one another.
As limbs posture.
And say nothing to one another.
They call my name.
It's my turn.

There's a new Fellow here.
Quiet.
They're all interested in my case.
Am I that complex ?
No.
It's just me.

I agree to try the botulinum toxin injections again.
A very different technique is used this time.
Once again I sense competence and commitment.
There's passion for dystonia here.
I'm part of it.
The shots hurt.
Are they supposed to ?
I begin to dread this procedure every three months.
I hate needles.

Despite the fact that I'm a nurse.

Dystonia is . . .

Elation.
The toxin worked.
I feel normal.
I had forgotten what normal "feels" like.
I must admit it does feel wonderful.
To simply be straight.
And not have to use sensory tricks.
That make others stare and laugh at you.
I can ride my bicycle again.
Freedom for me.
Success.
I head towards Central Park immediately.

Dystonia is . . .

The abnormal postures have returned.
I resent it.
Fixed postures.
I fall down a flight of stairs.
It happened at work.
Quite unexpectedly.
I feel angry at what dystonia does to me.
My friends try to comfort me.
But to no avail.
I only feel pain.
All due to dystonia.

Dystonia is . . .

The Letter.
Stating acceptance into medical school.

BEKA SERDANS, RN

A dream come true for me.
But how feasible is this ?
I knew I was " in" after the interview.
The interview fell during the peak toxin time effect range.
I was normal.
I looked straight.
Only during the interview.
I've done it and I'm immensely pleased.
My father always did tell me I would get "in" somehow.
Those were his last words to me.
What does the future hold for me ?
With dystonia ?

Dystonia is . . .

Six weeks have passed.
The toxin is wearing off.
It's supposed to last longer.
I'm disappointed.
Were the right muscles injected ?
May be not ?
The next time will be better.
I rationalize.
Thinking about the Letter.

Dystonia is . . .

I'm confused.
I've hit the "it's true I have dystonia" phase.
I feel the full impact of dystonia.
Success and failures.
I'm being tortured by dystonia and its effects.
How am I going to complete medical school ?
With this ?
With dystonia ?

I'M MOVING TWO

How am I going to pay for medical school ?
I watch the effects of the new health care reforms.
It's all money and business.
It's power.
It's Health Maintenance Organizations.
It's the denial of health care.
I can't compete.
I can't give 110% in this type of health-care setting.

I'm run down.
I worry.
I hate dystonia.

I've made my decision.
A wise decision.
I have been crying for a week.
Medical school is out of the question.
Out of my future.
Forever.
I sense disappointment from others.
I feel relieved.
They're not in my shoes.
Will I have any regrets ?
Only time will tell.

Dystonia is . . .

LOSS.
Loss of a dream.
Of hopes and plans for the future.
Disappointment.

Dystonia is . . .

Cervical dystonia, another name for torticollis.

A focal form.
A form of dystonia affecting a single part of the body.
Spontaneous remissions do occur.
Focal dystonias can progress.
Will I progress ?

Dystonia is . . .

I can't ride my bicycle anymore.
Maintaining balance is a problem.
But I can ride a four legged animal.
I met Taffy today.
A 27 year old geriatric tan colored mare.
A rather unmotivated creature.
I have a 3 hour date with a horse !
I don't know whose rear-end was heavier ?
Mine or hers ?
It took 15 minutes to climb aboard her.
No falls.
No worries about maintaining my balance.
We galloped endlessly.
I tired her out.
I feel refreshed.
I have another new hobby.
Involving horses.

Dystonia is . . .

Botulinum toxin-a denaturing agent.
A single protein chain known to STOP muscle contractions.
Hence, dystonia relief.
Is there really ever any relief from dystonia ?
You wake up with it.
You fall asleep with it.
It never leaves.

I'M MOVING TWO

You hope that it would.

Dystonia is . . .

Pasta, pasta, pasta . . .
Is this my favorite food ?
I'm eating out today.
People stare as I enter the restaurant.
I twist and turn.
I glare at them.
They look the other way.
But I still feel their stares as I sit down.
Silent stares.
We order entrees.
I order pasta.
We order dinner.
I order pasta.
No swallowing difficulties.
But the stares continue as I leave.
Pasta in hand !

Dystonia is . . .

Another visit with the famous neurologist.
What should I expect today ?
I feel clumsy today.
I struggle along.
Weaving among a crowd.
Will I reach the office ?
I have much to say.
A million questions to ask.
Many of which will have no answers.

WHY ?

Why do I have dystonia ?
Why is it not getting better ?
Why aren't things working ?
Why me ??

Some of my counterparts have already arrived.
Books in hand.
Traffic was tight this morning.
I eat a banana as I sit and wait.
Scribbling last minute notes.

A 30 minute neurological exam.
Not a 4-minute one.
Once again I sense competence.
I also sense concern.
There's five of them today.
Five physicians- all trying interpret my signs and symptoms.
Symptoms that are abnormal.
This I know.
This is all I know.
This all I want to know.

They leave the examining room.
They discuss their findings amongst themselves.
They forget that a person sits and waits.
In a room with four white walls.

A person with abnormal signs and symptoms.
I'm afraid.

Quietly they file back into the room.
Carrying in a heaviness into the room.
Have I done something wrong ?
My intuition as a nurse forewarns me.
I need more tests.

Neurological tests.
What does this mean ?
Why ?
I hear no answers.

I re-enter Fifth Avenue pondering.
I leave New York frightened.
No one hears me cry silently.

I feel numb for a week.
And restless.
The beach beckons me.
I stumble towards it.
Rather eagerly.
To drag out a drifting piece of dark-soaked bark.

Dystonia is . . .

A transition.
I've lost interest.
Interest in battling this disease.
I'm not going to win.
I'm disorganized.
I feel misdirected.
Misled by a disease.
That has no answers.

Dystonia is . . .

A new drug is prescribed.
One that is supposed to reduce spasticity.
Spasticity associated with dystonia.
Another treatment option.
There are many for dystonia.
Some have side-effects.

BEKA SERDANS, RN

The most common being drowsiness.
I plan all my activities now.
I look forward to a cure.
I look forward to the future.
And to LIFE.
Life without spasticity.

Dystonia is . . .

Demystifying Dystonia.
I've been searching.
Searching for appealing patient literature.
There is none.
None that commands attention.
None that comes from the heart.
None written by a person with dystonia.
None written by an RN with dystonia.

I have an idea.
It's Demystifying Dystonia.

Dystonia is . . .

Failure.
The toxin is no longer working.
I'm worse.
This I know.
No one else does.
But me.

Dystonia is . . .

Grief.
The emotional reaction to loss.

Mourning.
The active work involved in responding to loss.
Loss.
A state of being without something.

Dystonia is . . .

Loss of control.
Loss of self-image.
Loss of self-worth or self-value.
Loss of function.
Loss of "what was" and "what was to be".
Loss of self-purpose.

Dystonia is . . .

I have grieved.
I have mourned.
I have lost.
But I have gained.
I have discovered myself.
I think.

Dystonia is . . .

What is it?
This my colleagues ask.
They're interested.
They want to know.
I begin with flyers.
Posting dystonia flyers everywhere in the facility.
I wait for a response.
One comes.
Then another.
I begin to teach the basic facts of dystonia.

Using myself as an example.
They all listen.
And they finally applaud.
Dystonia is no longer unfamiliar to others.

Dystonia is . . .

I hear thunder.
I feel rain.
I want to help others with dystonia.
I want to give.

I have much to offer.
But to whom ?
Where ?
And how ?
I want to contribute.
Regardless of my symptoms.
Or the fact that the head moves only in one direction.
The left.

Dystonia is . . .

Photographs.
I sift through them.
I see myself.
I don't recognize myself.
"Is that me ?" I ask myself.
I'm no longer the same individual.
Yesterdays are gone.
Never to return.
Acceptance.
Dystonia is part of me.
Peace.
Has it really arrived yet ?

I'M MOVING TWO

Finally.
Eventually.
It will come for all.

Dystonia is . . .

RENEWAL
In one form or another.

Dystonia is . . .

The checkout line at the market is long.
Too long.
How long will I have to wait ?
It's sunny outside.
I grow impatient.
I'm in the correct aisle.
7 items in the 7 item checkout line.
How much longer ?
I begin to move forward.
Slowly.
As my lettuce begins to wilt.
I begin to wilt.
I wait and wonder.

Scientists have identified the dystonia gene.
The link to disease transmission.
Will a cure now be reality ?
I wait and wonder.
As my lettuce wilts.

A cure will lessen the need for experimentation.
There will be failures.
There will be successes.
There will be disappointments.

BEKA SERDANS, RN

A cure may not be total.
A cure may not be instant.
A cure may not be without problems.
A cure is a desire.
To escape from the realities of dystonia.

Dystonia is . . .

Dystonic.
Disease labeling.
I'm not dystonic.
I'm not a label.
I do not want to be known as a dystonic.
I'm a person.
An individual.

Labels dictate how one acts, feels and lives.
To live by a label only allows one to live by a set of symptoms.
A set of symptoms that reflect dystonia.
Not ME.

Dystonia is . . .

Accepting feelings.
Feelings that may arise within you.
Feelings that you may not be able to control.
Feelings that may develop slowly over time.
Feelings that may develop at unexpected times.
Without warning.
They all apply to dystonia.
And any other life experience.

Dystonia is . . .

The emotional phases of dystonia.
Shock.
Disbelief-Denial.
Bargaining.
Anger.
Confusion.
Why ?
Expectations.
Preoccupation.
Guilt.
Bitterness.
Envy.
In-Limbo.
Reality.
Struggle with new life patterns.
Life is worth LIVING.
These are the phases of any chronic disease.
Including dystonia.

A journey that all must enter.
A journey that I have entered and will complete.

Dystonia is . . .

Another office visit.
They need a team here.
A multi-dimensional approach to the treatment of this disease.
Dystonia is multi-dimensional.
It makes sense !
Do they know this ?
I wish they did.
It would help.

I dread these shots.
I don't look forward to them.
I only look forward to the beneficial effects of the toxin.
We all do.

They're going to use the electromyography machine.
More needles.
I dread this even more.
As my palms sweat.
And I fidget in the blue chair.
By using a needle electrode, the activity of an overactive muscle can be recorded.
I hear "sizzling","cooking popcorn" ,and "static-like" noises from the machine.
I expect the toxin to be injected in these areas.
My expectations come true.
The toxin is in.
A sigh of relief
Palms being dry.

Dystonia is . . .

Another 12 hour shift at work.
It's the night shift.
My colleagues ask me "how I am as I enter the unit ?"
I say "OK".
They question me again.
Do I not look OK ?
What am I supposed to say ?
The truth?
I admit tonight "I'm not OK."
I begin explaining.
The ravages of this disease.
That eats away at you.
They try to understand but they don't.

I have good days and bad days.
Tonight is a bad one.
I don't know why.
So how does one explain this ?
By simply saying "I'm OK."
And forgetting about things.

Dystonia is . . .

I've met someone.
Someone with dystonia.
I saw her leaning against the wall.
Her head tilts to the right.
She tries to straighten out but her body won't allow it.
I see myself in her.

She's 42 and has 3 kids.
She's had it for 4 years.
She takes medication.
It works.
But she's never met anyone else with dystonia.
We compare notes and our symptoms.
There are similarities.
There's a bond.
It's called dystonia.

Dystonia is . . .

Enmeshment.
Roles of family members become unclear.
Dependency may prevail.
Overprotectiveness.
Family members try to protect the person with dystonia .
They try to minimize the pain and reality of the disease.
Rigidity.

All try to maintain the status quo of the family.
It's called "maintaining a sense of normalcy."
Avoidance.
The signs and symptoms of dystonia are kept out of view.
Is dystonia a family disease ?
This I do not know.

Recommendations.
Don't blame dystonia on everything that goes on in your family.
Keep dystonia in perspective.
Learn how and when to confront problems.
Be realistic.
Be tolerant, consistent and flexible.
Talk about dystonia.
Educate your family about dystonia and how it affects YOU.
LIVE with dystonia, NOT FOR dystonia.

Simple advice.
But at times difficult to follow.
This I know.

Dystonia is . . .

I've been on a roller-coaster ride.
An emotional one as well as a physical one.
The toxin didn't work this time.
Absolutely no beneficial effects acquired this time.
I'm disappointed.
What will I do now ?
Do I have antibodies to the toxin ?
I hope not.
Things will be awful then.
They'll be worse.
Maybe I just need a bigger dose of the toxin ?

Another office visit.
Will it be a routine one ?
Like buying gasoline ?

I explain my story.
The toxin didn't work.
They agree.
I have antibodies to the toxin.
This is disappointing.
They say it's frustrating.   .
For whom ?
Them or me ?   .
I'm the one with the disease.
Not them.

We begin planning.
Planning new treatment options.
Many still exist.
They sound hopeful.
I don't know what to think.
Right now I feel powerless.
Over a disease that seems to control me.
It shouldn't be this way.
But it is.
This is the reality of dystonia.

Dystonia is . . .

Blue water.
Crystal clear waves.
Sandy beaches.
Heat without humidity.
Sun and surf.
Is this a cruise ship promotion ?

I'm on Lake Ontario.
Jet-skiing.
With friends.
This is exhilarating.
I don't want the day to end.
I've forgotten my disappointing news.
Antibodies.
I've forgotten dystonia.
And it's exhilarating.

Dystonia is . . .

He's 29.
He has Non-Hodgkin's Lymphoma.
He's married.
He has a beautiful two week old daughter.
A daughter who looks just like him.
With a mass of dark hair.
He's receiving massive amounts of chemotherapy.
He's not doing well.
But he's calm.
Waiting for a bone marrow transplant.
He's my patient.
And time is running out.
Slowly.
He teaches me.
A lesson that all need to learn and hear.
A lesson not spoken in words.
A lesson of utmost importance.
A lesson that spoken silently.
Life should be valued.
It can be taken away.
Never to be returned.

I realize that other people are in worse circumstances.
They are the ones who often teach us.
About the true meaning of LIFE.

Dystonia is . . .

Demystifying Dystonia.
It's completed.
All 45 pages.
It's a guide for others.
A guide to increase knowledge.
To decrease the sense of powerlessness.
To increase active participation.
To increase a sense of control.
It's a guide for others with dystonia.
It's called Demystifying Dystonia.

Dystonia is . . .

The Intensive Care Unit.
I've worked there for ten years.
My entire nursing career.
In one facility.
I'm sure that by now I've become a fixture.
It's a fourteen bed unit.
Reserved for the most critically ill.
Each room being encased in glass.
Four walls of glass.
Glass that constantly reminds me of dystonia.
Mirrors are worse reminders.
For a visual disease.

Dystonia is . . .

Shattering.
To ones former life.
To ones past life.
And to ones future life.
But we really need to start focusing on shattering dystonia.
And the associated stigma of it.

Dystonia is . . .

Verification.
Yes, its been verified.
I've developed antibodies to the botulinum toxin.
The poison that works for dystonia.
For whose dystonia ?
Not mine.
I was hoping that we would avoid this.
Once antibodies form, the effectiveness of botulinum toxin is
abolished.
Forever.

We all sit silently in the examining room.
The physicians and I.
I want to ask "why ?"
Why me ?
I only had six treatments.
Why ?
Why me ?

There is no answer.
Only silence.
Heavy disappointment lingers in the air.
For all who are involved in my dystonia management plan.

It was short-lived hope.
Was it really hope ?

I hate dystonia.
A disease without hope.
A disease with success and failures.
The development of antibodies is just one of those failures.

Dystonia is . . .

Two am.
Frau O. is awake.
I'm awake as furniture scrapes up above me.
BMW commercials seep through the ceiling.
She lives alone.
In the apartment above me.
She's 85.
And she should be in bed.
I'm too lazy to tap on the ceiling.
Asking for quietness.
My muscles ache.
I want to sleep.
My muscles seem to be on fire tonight.
Too much red wine.

Six am arrives as do the bicycles outside the University.
As I drift off to sleep.
To the sound of BMW commercials.

Dystonia is . . .

An activist.
An individual who wants to bring about change.
A change agent.
I come from a family of well-known Latvian activists.

Latvia.
One of three nations bordering the Baltic Sea.
Each being the size of the state of Virginia.
A nation known in Europe for its tremendous supply of amber.
A nation occupied by the Soviet Union in the 1940's.
Independent since 1990.
Rightfully so.
Yes, I'm a Latvian activist to a degree.
Now, it's time for me to become an activist for dystonia.
To change the Movement Disorder World.
We're not puppets.
But people.

Dystonia is . . .

I feel caged in today.
By a disease with no known cure.
A disease that begins with the fourth letter of the English alphabet.
Its symptoms entrap me.
I want to run and hide.
To escape.
To be free.
Free of the constant twisting and turning.
These are things that I cannot control.
Each day I am the lock.
Each day.
I want to face my opponent.
I want to stand tall.
Stand straight like a door does when opened.
And not run and hide.
From dystonia.
I try.
Every single day.

Sometimes it is an effort.
I never seem to win.
I can't find the key to the cage or the door.
But every day I continue looking for it.

Dystonia is . . .

I've entered the Land of Scarves.
Germany.
It's Fall.
The beginning of Golden October.
They love wearing scarves here.
And so do I.
They come in all sorts of styles ,shapes, lengths and colors.
They're perfect for those of us with deviated necks.
They hide deformities well.
And they're also very flattering.
To European men !
And one's own self image.

Dystonia is . . .

Karstadt.
The "Bloomingdales" of Munster.
It's a cool and rainy Saturday.
A constant stream of people flow through the swinging doors.
All congregate in the candy department area.
Bins of candy line the aisle.
Similar to a beverage drink aisle.
It's the main attraction of Karstadt.
I join them.
Among the chocolates.
There's Swiss, French, Italian, German, and Swedish varieties.
They're all delicious.
I've tried them all.

I locate the designated Swedish Fish area.
There are twenty varieties.
So many choices.
So many shades of color.
People begin milling around me.
I need to choose quickly.
Is dystonia a choice-less disease ?
Literature reinforces promising new treatments.
I left New York with vague choices.
Not sure what my choices were ?
Temporarily I choose a mixed batch of Swedish Fish.

Dystonia is . . .

The flight overseas was tolerable.
No one sat next to me.
I spent the entire flight in the horizontal position.
I had hoped it would turn out that way.
For some reason my body does not like the vertical position.
It does sound ridiculous.
But it is true.

Dystonia is . . .

My bicycle has been sitting in the basement.
It's still Golden October.
Inviting weather.
Perfect for my favorite hobby.
My neck seems OK.
Should I give it a try ?
Why not ?
Everyone else is.
The bicycle lanes aren't that heavily populated.
I should be OK.
I don't think I'll run into anything.

I adjust the seat.
Check the brakes.
And swing aboard.

I'm a bit wobbly.
As I reach the outskirts of my town.
I'm simply out of shape.
I hear someone chasing me down.
On my right side.
A fellow bicyclist.

Oops..Yikes.
I tumble into a metal fence that came out of nowhere.
No broken bones.
Except for a pair of torn Levis jeans.
I admit I had a slight problem with steering.
I must have looked silly on the road.
But then I look a bit silly doing just about everything.
Including bicycling.
A passion of mine.
Or a passion that once was.

I head for home.
A bit shaken up.
Using my own two feet.

Dystonia is . . .

I saw two people with dystonia.
One person had a head tremor.
The other had limb dystonia.
I watched them from the checkout line.
Actually I stared at them.
And probably made them extremely uncomfortable.

I know.
I've been in this same position also.

I should have introduced myself to them.
But it's tiring.
There are days when I don't want to discuss dystonia with anyone.
Today is such a day.
This is OK.
And one should acknowledge this.
We all need a break from dystonia.
There is always a time to talk about it.
And a time when it does not need to be spoken about.
Today I simply want to survive.
And not sink.

Dystonia is . . .

Returned to New York.
Another office visit.
What should I expect this time ?
The last time I was introduced to the concepts of biofeedback.
As a treatment form for dystonia.
It's not for me.
How can one convey this ?
It may work for some.
But not me.

There's another Fellow here.
She's got a heavenly British accent.
I wonder if she's an "afternoon tea and biscuit" individual ?
A sign of British origin.
It's quiet.
I'm the last patient in the office at 6 PM.
There's a patient sitting across the hallway from me.
I hear noises.Is it nervousness ?

Three physicians left her in the room.
To discuss their findings amongst themselves.
Enhancing loneliness.
For me and her.
The patient across the hallway.

It remains quiet.
And I'm the last patient.
For the day.
Time passes quickly.
We discuss my symptoms.
We're always discussing things.
Why not do something ?
Treat me.
Fix me.
An impossible request.
What's on the agenda ?
They say "the pathophysiology of your neck".
I don't care about this.
I want relief.
I want a treatment that works for me.
Is there one ?
They suggest biofeedback.
I want to laugh.
I do.
I remind them of the days of "levitation trials" held at slumber
parties in the 70's ?
I do.
I thought the trials were ridiculous.
I usually ruined the "trials" for everyone else.
Because I found them incredibly funny.
And I never could stop laughing.
Always ending up on the floor.

BEKA SERDANS, RN

I have a treatment suggestion - laughter.
It does wonders to the body.

I reenter Central Park again.
Not knowing where things from a dystonia point of view are going.

Dystonia is . . .

He was only 29.
He had Non-Hodgkin Lymphoma.
A type of cancer.
He had a 2 month old daughter.
And now he's gone.
Death.
Another phase of life.
A phase that brings grief and loss to many.
He taught me much.
And I feel honored that he did.
I'm sure a memorial fund will be established in his name.

Dystonia is . . .

Beka's back.
In the Intensive Care Unit.
Things have not changed.
But the patient population has.
Health Care Reform has entered New York State.
And it's frightening.
Where are we going ?
My job as a nurse may be on the line.
Overall, health care will be on the line.
Merges.
Downsizing.
Competition.
Those are the key words today.

And it's an unsettling feeling.
I wonder whether I will be entering the unemployment line?
Will I be one of those to be laid off?
I hope not.
Hopefully, my dystonia will not impact on employment issues.
It hasn't so far.

Dystonia is . . .

It's been incredibly busy in the ICU.
Some of us have been working about 50 hours a week.
There have been several patients who have clearly exhibited
dystonic signs.
I wonder whether dystonia is actually more prevalent than what is
being reported.

Dystonia is . . .

Its been raining non-stop for three days.
My garden is a mess.
My vacation is over.
Dystonia remains.
I had thought that it would go away.
But it didn't.
It's here to stay.
I fell into denial.
For a short while.
A phase that I thought I had already completed.
I'm learning.
It's all cyclical.
One enters a phase only to eventually return to it.
One cannot complete the journey.
One learns to live through the journey.
A journey of grief, loss, and dystonia.
Learning to live with this disease is only the beginning.

And I think that I've just begun.
Just as my garden will begin a new growth cycle in this anticipated
Spring.

Dystonia is . . .

Another office visit.
This is turning into a routine.
The waiting room is crowded once again.

I've been conversing with several other patients.
We are always comparing symptoms and treatment options with
one another.

I've turned into a temporary movie star.
I'm being video-taped again.
I'm not embarrassed.
May be it will provide some clues ?
On how to treat me.
I've developed a rather resistant form of dystonia.
They ask me to write "today is a sunny day".
Instead I write "Today is not a sunny day".
I'm exhausted.

My mind is exhausted.
A gentleman in the waiting room gave me his entire medical
history.
Over a 45 minute period.
He even showed me a copy of his electrocardiogram.

The video-taping finally stops.
What treatment options are there for me ?
This is all I want to know.
I hear of a new drug.
Should we try it ?

I'M MOVING TWO

68-SERD

Dystonia is . . .

There's a local dystonia support group meeting today.
And I'm going to attend it.
I've felt rather ambivalent about attending these meetings.
I don't know why.
I have been rather busy.
With two jobs.
As a nurse.

Still in the Intensive Care Unit.
I haven't quit yet.
Although I've been close to doing so.
The physical aspect of nursing is a load.
It can be tremendous at times.
Especially when there aren't enough of you around.
My colleagues are more run down than I.
I'm no longer the only one who leaves the unit feeling like a
"dishrag".
For the most part I've still been able to keep up with the pace in
the ICU.
I think I surprise my colleagues.
On a daily basis.
Considering that my dystonia interferes with things at times.

It's been so busy lately.
Patients are being admitted to the ICU at a rapid rate.
Sometimes it seems like they're knocking on our doors constantly.
Even when there are no more beds available.
Most of them arrive quickly.
To only leave slowly.
Some arrive in horrible shape.
Especially those with chronic diseases.
Like diabetes.

BEKA SERDANS, RN

I wish people would understand the importance of good health.
It means following certain restrictions sometimes.
It would help if people only listened.
To their health-care professionals.
To their symptoms.
Families pace in the waiting room.
Others camp out.
All hoping for the best outcome.

Some grieve.
Others laugh.
Not realizing the seriousness of their loved one's illness.
There's usually a pretty good reason for being admitted to the ICU.
Others save their tears for another time.
It's not easy.
Some wonder whether or not they'll make it through another day.
You always do.
But we all question this when faced with a "crisis".
Crisis always makes us learn to be strong.
To be tough.
To handle things.
In one way or another.
Often it takes time to recognize this.
Time can teach us much.

For now it has taught some of us "how to work 50 hours a week in the ICU".
A trend that doesn't appear to be slowing down.
For me.
Or any of my colleagues.

My other job is one that involves research.
On a Neurology Unit.
Just what I need.

When I live with a neurological disorder.
That is difficult to manage.

But this job I like.
Immensely so.
It involves analytical thinking.
Problem-solving.
Freedom.
Independence.
My boss treats me as one of her contemporaries.
She says I should get a Ph.D. in research.
I'd like to but not at the local university.
I belong elsewhere.
I want use my head instead of my body.
Dystonia relief to a certain degree.
Intelligence.
An item of value as is common sense.
I've been looking for a full-time research job.
No such luck yet.
Anywhere.

Dystonia is . . .

The meeting begins.
There are only four of us present.
Not too many.
Where are the rest ?
The group leader is a seasoned dystonia veteran.
Committed to a cause.
To help others.
With the same disease.
The cause needs more people like me.

I still want to help others.
Who are in the same situation as I.

I'd like to become a "movement disorder nurse clinician".
A nurse who specializes in movement disorders.
At a Movement Disorder Center.
Many would benefit from this.
I have all the skills.
But most of all I have the commitment needed for the position.
I have so many ideas.
But for now I'm told that there isn't any money to fund the position.
Is there anyone out there ?
With the funds ?
I have to start looking.

A cure for dystonia will not be found without funds.
To support research and education.
How can we make things happen ?
This is the focus of our meeting.
How do we rally the troops ?
Where do I look for the funds needed to implement my proposed position ?
I first need to find people willing to take a chance with the position.
To take a chance with me.
And a position that is much needed.
But it's valuable service has yet to be recognized

Dystonia is . . .

It's late Spring.
But it feels like early Fall.
I'm spending the day with L.
One of my best friends.
We met more than seven years ago in the ICU.
She had been there for four years before I came along.
We've been best friends since then.
Both of us have chronic diseases.

Both starting with the letter "D".
She has Diabetes.
I've got Dystonia.

We've had long conversations about both diseases.
You see, both of us have a disease that others have.
But we're also in the health-care business.
So, each of us can offer things that others in our field can't provide
to their patients.
Some try to put themselves in our shoes.
But let me tell you, some of them should stop trying.
It doesn't work always.

Both of us are waiting for the "big cures".
L.'s been waiting for 9 years.
I'm going into year 4.
Will a cure come ?
What do we do in the mean time ?
Sit and wait ?

Survive.
Each day.
D's are survivable.

The day is spent "flower-hunting".
Yes, both of us are gardeners.
L.'s looking for an "obedient plant".
I'm simply looking.
Wishing that my garden resembled those found in the issues of
Better Homes&Gardens.

Dystonia is . . .

Another day in the ICU.
I'm going into my 52nd hour.

BEKA SERDANS, RN

For the week.
I've got another 11 to go.
The shift has just started.
Everyone is on "edge".

I find out my boss is leaving.
For another nursing opportunity.
Elsewhere.
The unit is in-limbo.
I try not think about what the future holds.
For the ICU.
For me.
I strive to give 110% to my patients.
I always do.
Despite being on "edge".
For only today.

Things will change once again.
Change never ceases.
There are always adjustments to be made.
On a daily basis.
Is this good or bad ?
It's a question I need to ask God about.
There is no doubt that my dystonia has changed.
It has a mind of its own.
Separate from mine.
It's been incredibly resistant to treatment.
I wonder.
Do I really have dystonia ?
Or is it something else ?

I can no longer turn my head to the right at all.
Without the use of my hands.
Driving is nearly impossible.
I've put myself on self-imposed driving restrictions.

I avoid heavy traffic.
I use my own two feet.

Dystonia is . . .

The Taco Bell issue.
Taco Neck Syndrome.
I'm still thinking about this.
Many of my counterparts are in an uproar.
About the television commercials.
Featuring a sports figure.
Shaq O'Niel.
Actually I think the commercials are pretty clever.
Considering that they were developed by people without medical
degrees.
Who had no idea that dystonia even existed.

Dystonia is . . .

Blue sky.
For three days.
My garden is finally blooming.
Yellow and violet blooms predominate.
Tall and graceful.
Many they are.
Always reaching for the sky.
A blue sky.
With inviting cotton-shaped clouds.
That look ready for sitting.

Dystonia is . . .

I had a conversation today.
With my father.
At the cemetery.

Today.
My sister's wedding is next week.
Prior to my leaving for Europe.
So I've been thinking about him a lot lately.

I often wonder what he would think about everything.
About medical school.
About dystonia.
About me.
He always said "I had a brilliant mind".
That it would be put to good use somehow.
There have been times that my brilliant mind has gotten me in trouble.

My thoughts drift upwards towards him.
What he thought about himself ?
And his disease.
He had a tumor wrapped around his neck.
And elsewhere.
The lung, liver and spine.
All were inoperable at the time of diagnosis.
Prior to his death he became wheelchair-bound.
And housebound.
As a paraplegic.

He coped with the disease.
Often by himself in silence and dignity.
As things got worse.
He relied on his faith in God.
He would not talk very much about his disease.
My mother still does not understand this today.
Towards the end he became silent.
Not talking at all.
Everyone has their own way of coping with disease.
There is no right or wrong way.

As long as we attempt to cope.
That's what's important.
I would spend afternoons with him.
Reading.
Even if he slept.
I read him an entire book on Organic Chemistry.
A frequently disliked pre-med course.
From there we went on to Physics.
Another dreaded pre-med course.
I liked both of them.
Even though I had to self-educate myself in Calculus.
Still another dreaded pre-med course.

He always listened.
Despite being tired.
And being partially immobile.
From an unusual tumor.
That proved to be difficult to treat.
Physicians would have endless conferences.
On what to do.
And what not to do with him.

As I think of him.
I am reminded of how similar I am to him.
In coping styles.
As my dystonia worsens.
I too rely on my faith in God.

There are days when I still miss him.
One of those days will be my sister's wedding day.
But I must say this.
That although it was difficult to watch a parent die slowly.
It's an experience that allowed me to I find myself.
As a daughter.
As a nurse.

And as a person.
Our roads will cross again.
Some may not agree with these views.
But then they have not experienced what I have over the last seven years.
I have gained much from loss.
This is what life is all about.

Dystonia is . . .

Anticipation.
We've been cleaning the house.
And cooking.
As the wedding day draws closer.
There seems to be so much to do in so little time.

Dystonia is . . .

Temperature: 85 degrees.
Blue skies thrill us once again.
My daisies are thriving.
Some occupy the house.
In every room.
In clear crystal vases.
All bought at Ikea- the Swedish furniture store.

In eight days I leave for Europe.
Two weeks will be spent in Sweden.
Three in Germany.
As my aunt would say.
The countdown has begun.

Dystonia is . . .

I'm hanging out on the beach.

I'M MOVING TWO

With my first best friend.
M.J.
Also a nurse.
Who was not named after the candy.
In the yellow wrapper.
She dislikes any reference made towards them.
I, on the other hand, find them to be one of my favorites.
Easily finishing a handful in front of her.
We're two semi-invalids sitting on the beach.
And chuckling about it.
M.J just had major back surgery.
All due to heavy lifting.
We both suffer from spasms.
And laugh a lot.
Sometimes too much.

Dystonia is . . .

Chuckle, chuckle.

Dystonia is . . .

I drag my bicycle up from the basement today.
It hasn't been in use for awhile.
Nearly breaking a leg during the task.
Carrying it upstairs.

I try riding it.
But I fail.
For some reason I can't maintain my balance on it.
I don't know if it's the dystonia that's interfering with things.
What am I going to do ?
I have a bicycle waiting for me in Europe.
I begin to convince myself.
That today is just a bad day.

Of course, I know how to ride a bicycle.
Ever since age 5.
Tomorrow will be better.

I throw my bicycle back in the garage.
I don't want to see it.
Or to think that I probably can no longer ride it.
One of my past- hobbies.

So I can't drive.
I can't bicycle.
Time to figure something else out.
Taffy, my four-legged companion, has retired.
A 28 year old horse.
In retirement.
I'd like to retire.
Wouldn't we all ?

Dystonia is . . .

I'm taking orders.
Some of my colleagues in the ICU want "european stuff".
Wooden Swedish horses.
Swedish crystal.
Chocolate.
Birkenstocks.
The list seems to be getting longer.
Postcards.
Pictures.
Letters.
I tell them that I haven't moved there yet.
We chuckle.
All of them know about my European background.
They've given me a nickname.
Ms. Europa !

I'M MOVING TWO

What can I say ?
I just chuckle.
They know that they'll have to wait for their orders.
I'm shipping everything back to the US.
My neck and back can't handle the heavy load.
A 35 kg suitcase.
It will only aggravate the twisting and turning.

I haven't been able to move my shoulders.
My hands have been falling asleep.
Finding a comfortable sleeping position has been impossible at
times.
And there's been another problem.
That's a bit unnerving.
And unsettling.
There's a pulling sensation in the right leg.
That's how the neck began initially.
Only I know that it's there.
No one else knows.
But me.

I hate dystonia.
Especially when it worsens.

Is there any control over it ?
I think not.
At least in my case.
I don't want to rely on false hope.

Dystonia is . . .

These new symptoms couldn't happen at a better time.
Sarcasm.
The overseas flight is an 8 hour one.
The flight has been sold out.

For weeks.
I already know that I won't have an empty seat next to me.
The economy class section doesn't have a lot room for tall people.
Even on Lufthansa.
The section was devised by someone who was short.
Not tall.
Like me.
I have no idea how I am going to tolerate the flight.
Being cramped and all.
May be a German businessman will be willing to exchange their seat?
For me.
That's all I want.
Other than getting there in one piece.
A news magazine show reminded me of Flight TWA 800 last week.

I think of all those people on that flight.
One minute you're here.
The next you're not.
My heart feels heavy for those family members.

Therefore.
I shouldn't complain about my upcoming flight and how I'm going to tolerate it.
I'll tolerate it.
Somehow.

Dystonia is . . .

This is turning into a bad week.
I had another "fender-bender".
My second one.
If I don't kill myself or someone else while I'm driving.
My doctor will when he finds out about this.

I'M MOVING TWO

I'm well aware that I shouldn't be driving.
But how am I supposed to get around ?
This isn't Europe or even Boston.

I don't know what happened.
I was turning to the right.
And this other vehicle came out of nowhere.
I was handed a ticket.
My third one in the last two years.
So I don't exactly have a clean driving record anymore.

I was shaken up a bit.
I kept my composure during the ticket write-up.
But the reality of dystonia struck again.
As I headed for home.
Crying.

I got quite a lecture from L. regarding this latest event.
At least I won't be driving on the German Autobahn.

Dystonia is . . .

I fell into a shallow roadside ravine today.
The ravine was overflowing with wild phlox.
Purple ones.
They bloom most of the summer.
And need very little care.
From a gardener.
I had to dig some of them up for my garden.
They were free simply waiting for someone to arrive and admire
them.
I'll admire them in my garden.
I had to have some.
Instead I found myself in a ravine.

Filled with phlox.
Not a good week.

Dystonia is . . .

Father's Day.
Silence.

The countdown has ended.
I'm heading off to Europe.
My second home.
My sister's wedding was a success.
She's happy.

I leave for Europe in two days.
Time to start packing.
As little as possible.
The less I have to carry the better for me.
Less neck strain.

The 19th of July has arrived.
I head off to New York.
My journey has begun.
Excitement fills the senses.
As do dreams of Sweden.
My mother giving me an update on Sweden.

Dystonia is . . .

The flight was long.
A person sat next to me.
He climbed over me to get to the aisle about 7 times.
Rather than asking me to step aside first.
He reminded me of a gorilla.
At least the climbing did !

After a six hour flight.
I was glad to get off the plane.
I did so rather quickly.
Escaping from the gorilla.

Dystonia is . . .

Impressions of a Swedish Summer.
The Stockholm Archipelago.
A string of 24,000 islands along Sweden's East coast.
1,000 inhabited islands.
With 6,000 permanent residents.
3,900 square miles.
Home to birds, fish and seals.
A few hardy fishermen live on the isles.
Wildflowers bloom along rocky crevasses.
Red painted houses predominate.
As do the Lupines.
Violet coexist with fuschia and pink colored ones.

Stockholm is the capital.
Easy to get around in.
One of the few cities where one can swim or fish.
In the downtown district.
In front of the Parliament building.
My mother did tell me about this.
She also warned me about "Nippon soppa".
She spent nine years living in Sweden.
After the war.

Nippon soppa is a "berry-like" drink.
The consistency of a cream soup.
Soppa means soup.
Several flavors exist.

My favorites are blueberry and one made of grinded rose petals.
The Swedes pride themselves with this drink.
It truly is quite delicious.
Especially over ice-cream.

I consume a liter of it everyday.
Over a two week period.

Beautiful walks along Stockholm's waterways.
Cool dips in the ocean.
Berry-picking.
Picking wildflowers.
Peace.
A good book.
Take up my time in Sweden.

Sweden's "inland sea".
Lake Malaren.
It sits in the middle of Sweden.
The core of Sweden's folk-life exists here.

The water crystals.
Clear blue.
Surrounded by fir trees.
We passed through endless fields of forests.
By train.
The air is clean.
And fresh.
Non-polluted.

Sweden.
An environment-conscious nation.
Lifestyles change according to seasons.
During summer one sleeps very little.

The "white nights" flourish.
Daylight does not seem to end.

We visit the Royal Palace.
Retracing historical roots.
The old city of Stockholm.
Crowded.
With tourists.
And antique shops.

The weather has been spectacular.
Sunshine each day.
Several cruises have been taken.
To Finland.
And the island of Gotland.
A mid-evil island.
The capital is Visby.
Surrounded by 12th century castle walls.
Climbing roses creep along residential streets.
What a sight !
I take plenty of pictures.
Over 100 Gothic churches remain within the city walls.
Gotland was the site for a Latvian Folk-Art-Choir Festival in 1989.

An afternoon is spent by the sea.
Basking in golden sunshine.
Dystonia forgotten.
Temporarily.

Kristenhammen.
Hallsberg.
Karlstad.
Malmo.
Uppsala.
A city known for neurology research.

Helsingborg.
Marienhamm.
Mora.
Aland.
Visby.
These are some of the places.
That we visit.
As we crisscross Sweden by rail.

Hennes&Mauritz.
The fashion store for most young Europeans.
Near my age.
I've gone on a shopping-spree.
The clothing that I've bought will definitely stand out.
In conservative Rochester.
What will my mother say ?
Most likely nothing.
She always says that I do things unlike others.
I never join a crowd.
Independent as always.
Reiterated by my father in the past.

I leave the store with a new wardrobe.
Wondering how am I going to carry it back to Munster ?
It's a 12 hour train-ride back.
From Stockholm.
To Munster.

The train ride back.
Has been long.
A day spent in Copenhagen.
Another city that sits on a group of islands.
I'm the ICU's jet-setter.
Envied by some.
Several ferry rides are needed to get back to Germany.

The ferries are also crowded.
Little room to move.
Once aboard everyone heads for the duty-free shops.
People leave the ferry carrying case loads of wine and other alcohol.
Alcohol is strictly controlled in the Scandinavian countries.
Sold at special stores.
Only during specific hours.
So, people leave the ferries with more than they can carry.
Suitcases, bags break as they rush down the exit planks.
Alcohol spilling on the gangways.
Back in Munster.
My second hometown.
A town filled with students.

It's Equestrian season.
The stables have been built.
To house the best horses in Germany.
For a five day event.

I've been wandering through the stables.
Looking for the horses.
The stables sit in front of the University Administrative offices.
My aunt works there.
Her boss is Herr K.
He and I have had long and interesting conversations.
About everything.
Including DeMystifying Dystonia.
He's trying to learn English.
Problems with the "ie's" and "ei's" exist.
I still have problems with English as well.

My aunt and I plan our next escapade.
Israel is a choice.
As well as the Austrian-Hungary Alps.
I want to go to both areas.

I've spent four wonderful weeks in Europe.
I don't want to return home.
But job obligations haunt me.

I found out that one of our retired surgeons and mentor.
Who recommended me for medical school.
Has been ill.
This is distressing.
I still often wonder "why do bad things happen to good people ?".
A question without clear answers.
This is part of life.
With all its ups and downs.

The world has become very automated.
We all run here and there trying to out do one another.
In one way or another.
We need to slow down.
And take stock of what we have.
Without trying to out-do one another.
Life is good.
Even with dystonia.

Dystonia is . . .

Sweltering heat.
Smoke.
Horns.
People.
Restlessness.
I've arrived back in New York.

Another appointment with the famous dystonia expert.
I arrive at the office without a list of questions.
I don't have much to say.

I'M MOVING TWO

Are there any new treatment options ?
Yes.
We try a new drug.
I hope it works.
I'm always hoping to only be disappointed later on.
Beka's back in the ICU.
I find out that half of the staff is leaving to go elsewhere.
This is disappointing.
And nerve-racking.
Do those of us who remain leave or stay ?
I feel restless.
I myself have been looking for a job elsewhere.
But cannot find one that will allow me to do what I can do.
To give to others with dystonia.
The needs of those with dystonia and other movement disorders
can be immense.
Many do not realize these needs.
Especially health-care professionals.
Who do not suffer from the disease.
But treat the disease only.
To the best of their abilities.

Mirroring.
Validating.
Empathizing.
These are things that many with dystonia need.
From their health-care professionals.
But no one is listening about these things yet.

Dystonia is . . .

Not much has changed in the ICU.
Except for the staff.
Everyone wants to see my European pictures.
There's over a hundred of them.

BEKA SERDANS, RN

Dystonia is . . .

Another neurology office visit.
I end up screaming at my neurologist.
Telling him he knows nothing about dystonia.
What a foolish thing to say.
Especially to the dystonia expert.
I hate dystonia.
Every drug that I try does nothing.
Walking has been difficult.
At times.
I'm afraid.
The use of my sensory tricks has increased.
I feel frustrated.
And restless.
Impatient.
I hear about the new dystonia gene.
The DYT1 gene.
Finally discovered.
A cure may be revealed in the near future.

I've been thinking about a group of medications that cause dystonia.
There are about 20 of them.
Someone should look at the chemical structures of these medications.
There are some similarities.
From an organic chemistry point of view.

I can't believe that I screamed at my neurologist.
But I'm tired of this disease.
A disease with progressive symptoms.
Beka lost it this time.
During an office visit.

However, by screaming I vented some anger.
Everyone with a chronic disease feels angry.
At some point.
I'm only human.
I apologize.
For my screaming.
Apology accepted.

I enter a research study.
A double-blind study.
I fill out forms.
And ask plenty of questions.
Before I sign a consent form.
And try another potential new treatment option for dystonia.

Dystonia is . . .

Nashville.
Home of Opryland.
Symposium time.
I meet many people with dystonia.
Many want to share their stories with me.
They've heard that I'm a nurse with dystonia.
For two days I listen.
To stories.
Symptoms.
Answering questions.
About medications and their side-effects.
About HMO's and health-care.
About other issues.
All related to dystonia.

I leave the symposium.
Having met many people with dystonia.
Listening to others has been good therapy for me.

BEKA SERDANS, RN

I was able to act as a patient advocate.
This is my role in the movement disorder world.

I realize that I'm quite resourceful.
Even with dystonia.

Dystonia is . . .

The El Nino effect predominates the news.
The effects are devastating to many.
As can be the effects of dystonia.
Overall during the last few weeks I've been doing reasonably well.
Driving is difficult though.
I find myself crisscrossing lanes at times.
Running red lights.
Speeding.
And doing a number of other ridiculous things.
With the steering wheel.
In order to drive straight.
Without the use of sensory tricks.

Chuckle, chuckle, chuckle.

Dystonia is . . .

Found myself in the newspaper twice over the last three weeks.
Even received a response from Newsweek magazine.
I've been on a writing campaign.
Writing to newspaper men, TV reporters etc.
Anywhere.
To raise awareness about dystonia and the need for funding.
Everyone needs to get involved.
Regardless of the effects of dystonia.

We can accomplish much.
If we all work together.

I've been getting a number of phone calls.
From others with varying degrees of dystonia.
I answer many of their questions.
But mostly, I listen to many of them.

This is what so many individuals need.
Many are isolated.
Lonely.
And desperate.
For help.
For a cure.
Isolated.

Dystonia is . . .

Another escape to Europe.
For three weeks.
I'm now 32.
And it's Christmas.
In Germany.

Snow.
Sleet.
Rain.
X-mas carols.
Printen.
A form of gingerbread.
Available everywhere.
We munch on it.
As we walk along the cobbled streets of Munster.
Sipping on Weinnachten wine.
A red hot German wine.

Many of our friends are back from Latvia.
Many from Munster spend several summer months there.
Each year.
It's a time to exchange stories.
To hear what's new on the political scene.

All want to know how my dystonia is.
What can I say ?
It's still there.
It certainly hasn't left.

I'm refocused.
A job awaits me in New York.
At an Upper Eastside hospital.
Another chapter in my life.

Dystonia is . . .

Resignation announcement.
My colleagues can't quite believe that I'm leaving.
I am.
For new opportunities.
New goals have been formulated.
No more shuttling.
For appropriate health-care.
Dystonia care.
It has been a burden for 3 years now.
Particularly, a financial one.

Relief.
Eager anticipation.
500 miles closer to Europe.

I'M MOVING TWO

Off to New York City.

Dystonia is . . .

I've been on a journey.
A long one.
Full of ups and downs.
I have struggled but I am not the first.
Nor the last.
The struggles will continue.
But I have rebuilt a new life.
A new life with dystonia.
It is different now.
I have reinvested in work, activities, family and friends.
I have developed new ways of living.
New options and possibilities exist for me.
They exist for all.
Ones that did not exist before dystonia.

Dystonia is . . .

I have lost yet I have gained.
I am stronger.
I am wiser.
I am more compassionate.
I am aware of the struggles of others.
I have evaluated old beliefs.
And developed new ones.
I have changed goals and sought new ones.
My philosophy of life has changed.
For the better.

I have found the meaning of life.
I have moved ahead.
Even with dystonia.

BEKA SERDANS, RN

We all can.
We all must.
Even with dystonia.

Dystonia is . . .

It's moving day.
The movers have arrived.
I watch and direct.
A mirror breaks.
It's replaceable.
This day has long been anticipated.
I'm not the least bit nervous.
About this.
Or anything.
Everything is packed in a matter of hours.
My movers drive off.
Heading towards Manhattan.
My apartment awaits me.
On the Upper East Side.

I found it in one day.
In a good and safe area.
A semi-studio.
Within walking distance of work.
No more driving.
A relief.
No more accidents.
Dystonia may now be less burdensome.
I hope.

My mother, sister and I arrive in my apartment.

Prior to the movers.
My mother is amazed at my lucky find.

I'M MOVING TWO

She likes the apartment.
Separate kitchen and bath.

We begin cleaning.
Starting with the bathroom.
Dirt and grime cover us within an hour.
By days end my mother throws out her clothing.
Despite the fact that everything shines.
And there was only one dead cockroach.

I meet my next door neighbor.
A Hungarian.
Short.
But rather quick on his feet.
From Budapest.
A city I hope to explore one day.
A city of many bridges.
And elegance.

We continue cleaning.
The movers arrive with all of my stuff.
26 boxes and all.
A futon.
Bookshelves.
And plenty of dry food.
Pasta and rice.

We begin arranging the furniture.
My mother having a knack for interior design.
Without a college degree.
My mother spent a number of years in Sweden.
Thus, the influence of Swedish design.
Wood, wood, wood.
Along with Carl Larsson paintings.
Which are arranged craftily in a matter of minutes.

My sister arranges my bookshelves and its readable contents.
Always intrigued by the number and quality.
A slow process.
As she sifts through pages and countless CDs.

Quite an opposite of me.
Strong and healthy.
Obtaining a degree in Communications.
From Boston University.
Half a foot taller than I.
Not as fine boned as I.
But a blonde.
With a brilliant smile.
A dedicated former member of BU's rowing team.
With extreme strength.
5 PM.
The apartment looks livable.
We go out to eat.
Plenty of pasta bars.
We finish the day in bed.
Watching Nightline.
Sipping on red wine.
As sleep creeps upon us.

By the end of the weekend I'm alone.
Wondering in disbelief that I'm in New York.
Of all places.
Five years ago I was planning on entering medical school.
A dream destroyed by dystonia.
Its symptoms continue.
Never abating.
A constant reminder.
Of unmet dreams.

I begin my new job.
Within a coronary care unit.
Progressive to a degree.
But certainly regressive from a nursing point of view.
Little orientation.
I meet a variety of individuals.
Some with a mission.
Others with little to offer their patients.

Weeks go by.
And I realize that my standards of nursing care are different.
Few among the staff carry standards.
Or do not recognize the value of standards.
Some do not carry any standards at all.
I see things that I cannot even write about.
Disturbing things.
That I eventually tell my endocrinologist about.
A wonderful physician.
Whom I trust.
I find out that I'm his second dystonia patient.
He has a sense of humor.
Always making you laugh.
He comprehends dystonia.
And is not offended by all the sensory tricks.
Some of which are unusual and unsettling.
Well versed on endocrinology.
A difficult sub-specialty.
Many chronic patients.
With diseases that affect all body systems.
That can be costly to current health-care systems.

Four weeks of the day shift are over.
I wonder how I managed.
Being a night person.
I return to the night shift.

A different set of co-workers.
Some young.
Others old.
Again I see things being done that shouldn't be done.
Few understand my dystonia.
Despite my explanations.
Which are lengthy but informative.
Many of the physicians listen.
And are intrigued by me.

I'm not that intriguing.
I'm simply being me.
I meet many patients as I strive to give good quality care.
The type of care that everyone deserves.
Compassionate care.
That meets standards.
And nothing less.
This causes friction amongst the staff.
Patient families begin asking for me.
To provide care to their loved ones.

And this upsets some co-workers.
Additional friction.
Muscle friction.
Something that I must face everyday.

Dystonia is . . .

Questions.
From my patients.
About my neck.
And the abnormal movements.
I describe dystonia to all who show an interest.
I have little support from my co-workers.
Disinterest exists.

Little empathy.
Not much concern.
Few questions.
I begin looking for a new job.
Elsewhere.
Away from an archaic style of nursing.

Dystonia is . . .

April.
Tulips bloom along Park Avenue.
I sit and watch taxis zoom by at rapid pace.
I'm uneasy.
And unhappy.
I miss my co-workers in Rochester.
The support.
Something everyone needs within their work environment.
I suspect that I'm "one of a kind".
Like my dystonia.

Dystonia is . . .

Once again I sit.
Waiting in my dystonia expert's office.
He greets me with a warm smile.
And a handshake.

Maintaining the physician-patient relationship.
One filled with compassion.
On his part.
I enter a new research trial.
I read 6 pages of information.
And sign the last page.
A mark of my commitment to research.

In a few days I write up a new brochure for the clinic.
Describing the research process.
In lay-mans terms.
For my counterparts.
The brochure is well received.
Could writing be a career for me ?
A question I begin to ponder.

Ideas come to mind in a matter of minutes.
And are quickly recreated on paper.
Intelligence.
This I have.
Writing skills.
This I also have.
But how does one make a living from these skills ?

It's botulinum toxin day.
The injections go in smoothly
I feel better within an hour.
I walk down Madison Ave.
Straight.
Looking normal.
And feeling jubilant.

Dystonia is . . .

Work is tiring.
I'm depressed.
I had not realized what a move entails.
From a place of familiarity.
To an area of the unknown.

Six weeks have gone by since the move.
Tears come and go.
My job is stressful.

I'M MOVING TWO

Co-workers are not "co-workers".
The definition of a "co-worker" is unfamiliar to the Unit.
I continue to see disturbing things.
Things that affect me.
Moralistically.

I begin to despise working.
In a cruel environment.
I become a victim.
Because of my high standards of nursing.
What can I do ?
With 11 years of critical care nursing I cannot change my standards.
Standards only lead to good care for others.
Isn't this what health-care is about ?

I write a letter of resignation.
Something I've never done before.
I call my friends for advice.
They all agree with my decision.

My letter is slipped under a door.
And accepted.
Relief for me.
I'm no longer a victim.
Of the cruelty of others.
Of silent discrimination.

Often people do not recognize the unnecessary hurt and pain that their behavior does to another.
Physical pain and hurt are quite different from that of mental pain and hurt.
Both can cause much distress to an individual.
Distress and pain already dominate the news.
Why have more ?

BEKA SERDANS, RN

I often wish it would stop.
One day it will.
It says so in the Bible.
I look forward to this day.
As do a few others who believe in the Word.

Dystonia is . . .

Another office visit.
These office visits are tiring.
As is dystonia.
I answer questions about my symptoms.
From a research coordinator.
Named S.
I like her immediately.
I talk her through "drawing a blood sample" from me.
Success.
My dystonia expert enters the room.
Clearly surprised that I'm instructing his research coordinator on
the process of phlebotomy.
A skill that takes practice.
I am a nurse after all.
And we're always giving instructions to patients and families.
It's time to sit straight in a chair.
To let the head do what it wants.
To drift to the left and downwards.
And be evaluated again.
Using the TWISTER Scales.
And a number of other scales.
That my mind cannot comprehend.
I tell my doctor this.
That there must be a simpler way of evaluating the effects of the
toxin.
Simpler forms and questions should be developed.
I do not know whether he wants to hear this from a patient.

But I'm only thinking of other patients.
The evaluation of research can be made simpler.
I leave the office more confused than ever.
Not knowing if the toxin worked or not.

Dystonia is . . .

I head back home for a number of weeks.
Summer has arrived.
My garden needs attention.
I spend hours mumbling to my plants.
Revamping the entire yard.
Utilizing drawing skills.
Basking in the sunshine.
Driving my car.
Without an accident.
I spend a number of days working in my old ICU.
Everyone listens to my New York stories.
Things have changed.
I'm still able to give 100% to my patients.
No questions asked.
I'm respected for my abilities.
The support has not disappeared.
Amongst the new merge.
Of H. and S.

Dystonia is . . .

The heat in my apartment is unforgivable.
My neighbor warned me about my apartment being the warmest.
But he also stated that I've got the best apartment on the floor.
He jingles his keys each morning.
As he walks to the local senior citizen center for a swim.
We always chit-chat in the laundry room.
He's never asked me about my neck.

I must look normal to him.
But then being a European.
One doesn't ask out-right questions to another person.
Out of respect for the other.

Instead of going to bed.
After a 12 hour shift.
I run to Gracious Homes to buy a fan.

Dystonia is . . .

DeMystifying Dystonia is finally available to others.
And turns out to be a huge success.
Not a surprise to me.
It is for others.
Including the dystonia expert.

An appointment with my endocrinologist.
A routine check-up.
We discuss "rat units instead of mouse units".
Botulinum toxin is given in mouse units.
Laughter and giggles fizzle in the office.
Some much needed laughter for me.
I've been feeling down in the dumps.
Regarding my dystonia.
The beneficial effects of the toxin last only 6 weeks.
Rather disappointing.
But a different strain of the toxin is being used.
Toxin A being the most potent.
Of six strains.
Named A, B, C, D, E and F.

It's almost August and I'm back home.
Sifting through my garden.
As my aunt tells me about her 5 week trip to Latvia.

Her first time back since leaving the country during World War II.
Her plane ride to Helsinki and then Riga was traumatic.
An experience for her.
At least she did not get stranded.
She met many relatives.
Some of whom I never knew existed.
But then Latvians have a habit of cropping up anywhere in the world.
There's only 2 million of us left in the entire world.
And I'm probably the only one with dystonia.
It seems that no one in my entire family has dystonia.
So, where did I get it from ?

I think the answer to this question lies in my mother's family.
You see, her father died at the age of 44 when my mother was only four.
In a German refugee camp within the British zone.
He had some sort of spinal problem.
Never clearly diagnosed.
Marked as an "auslander" by post-war Germans.
All non-Germans were regarded as this in the 1950's..
I think the dystonic link is tied with him.
His body is buried along the German-Dutch border.
None of us know where.
He's a grandparent I know very little about.
Having seen only a few pictures of him.

Dystonia is . . .

A genetic link for one type of dystonia is announced.
My own dystonia expert was part of the scientific team.
But then he seems to be part of every dystonia scientific team.
Always doing something for dystonia.
How does he find the time to do so much ?
Always striving.

BEKA SERDANS, RN

Reading.
Writing.
Examining.
And evaluating us with dystonia.
Is it commitment or disease obsession ?
Something I'm trying to figure out.
I'm working on it.
Rather slowly.

It is good to be dedicated to a cause, disease, or idea.
As long as one does not forget that life is meant to be lived.
Today.
Not tomorrow.
Too many people pass through life not having experienced what it
has to offer us.
Life is full of opportunities.
Some not to be missed.
One simply has to listen to God.
For the right direction.
He always knows which path is right for you.
Even when you do not know.
Relying on Him sometimes is the best thing.
But it does take patience.
And time.

I'm glad I'm in the hands of my dystonia expert.
Wouldn't trade him for a minute.

Dystonia is . . .

Time for another series of injections.
The toxin works within an hour.
Rather amazingly.

Dystonia is . . .

I begin my new job.
Floating amongst 5 different Intensive Care Units.
I find that I like the Neurological ICU the best.
Everyone in the unit recognizes dystonia.
Despite the recognition of the disease there are still plenty of
questions.
Which I answer eagerly.
No one including the physicians are put "off" by the dystonia.
I meet a CBS person.
Maybe I can convince them of the importance of the need for
awareness ?
For dystonia.
Television exposure.
At the national level.

Dystonia is . . .

NBC News.
Dateline, the news magazine, calls me.
An unexpected call.
They want to do a story on me and use of the toxin.
My letter campaign worked.
I did not give up.
I immediately call my friends.
Joy and excitement.
My dystonia expert is in "disbelief".
And wondering "how I did it ?".
I accomplished this goal by myself.
Never giving up.
One does not have to be a high ranking individual in society to
accomplish something.
When there is a will, there is a way.
I am pleased with myself.

Because this project will help so many others.
That is my wish.

I meet the producer.
Dressed in a well-fitted cream colored suit.
And the camera crew.
3 wonderful people.
Diligent in their craft.
We film in my apartment.

Eating in a upright fashion has been a problem.
The neck now rotates to the left and downwards as well.
How does one eat without using sensory tricks ?
The answer is in a flat position.
My dystonia is getting worse.
This is the pits.

Filming continues in Central Park.
In Rochester.
And then at The Essex Hotel.
For an interview.
An hour in length.
I arrive at the hotel not knowing what I will say.
The questions begin.
And amazement and respect intercede the interview.
The interview ends with the exchange of autographs.
I answered simply and honestly.
Even when the issue of a cure was brought up.
Do I foresee a cure within five years ?
My answer was NO.
Dystonia is an amazingly complex disease.
We actually know very little about it.
There is much to be learned about the disease.
A cure will help those who develop the disease in the future.
But will it help those of us suffering from the disease today ?

I worry about the care being given to those of us who currently
have the disease.
The disease carries with it depression, disability, chronic pain, self-
worth and self- image problems that are not being addressed in
office visits.
How does one cope with unemployment ?
Health-care insurance that does not cover treatments ?
Even I wonder how much longer I can continue working as a
critical care nurse.
Not a day passes when I do not think of this.
What will I do then ?
Where will I go ?
Do I simply give up like so many others have ?
Join the disability ranks ?
I worry about the emotional toil this disease can have on an
individual.
Research will improve the lives of those who are at risk for the
disease.
In the future.
But what about us ?
Us, today ?

Providing literature does not necessarily solve the problem.
Of us, today.
Centers need to establish programs that will assist us with daily
activities.
We are a long way from a cure.
I do not foresee a cure in five years.
Time moves quickly.
Even those with HIV are still waiting for a vaccine.
That was promised years ago.
This is not pessimistic thinking.
It's honest and realistic thinking.
Thinking that some may not agree with at all.

BEKA SERDANS, RN

And will anger some.
As they watch the segment.

But those who may feel angry do not have to deal with this disease.
On a daily basis.
Treating is quite different from living with the disease.
At that matter, any disease.

Dystonia is . . .

The Dateline crew arrives at the clinic.
I'm allowing them to film the injection process of botulinum toxin..
I hope that I don't scream during the process.
I focus on asking the film crew plenty of questions.
About the filming process.
And about broadcast production.

To no avail I cannot suppress the pain felt during the injections.
A dreadfully long needle is used.
The sound man listens to a lot of "ohhs and ahhs".
There must be a way to make the injection process of the toxin
more tolerable.

The dystonia expert finally believes me.
Dateline was in his clinic.
And is left once again wondering "how I did it ?".
News-magazines get hundreds of letters from individuals asking for
representation of a cause or idea.
One simply has to persevere and ask for God's help along the way.
He opens and closes doors.
This time he opened a door.
Rather unexpectedly.

I spend additional time with the film crew.
H. certainly is an expert in his craft.

A friendship is forged.
My bicycle is fixed.
Which I ride in Central Park.
During any tolerable weather.

The air date of the segment is held.
As the nation collects their thoughts on the definition of impeachment.

Dystonia is . . .

I head back home once again for Thanksgiving.   .
Terrible news.
My sister is getting a divorce.
I cry for her.
A heavy loss for her.
It is difficult.
And worsens my dystonia.
Something that I have no control over.
I end up eating a partially pureed Thanksgiving dinner.
I spend three weeks at home.
Being kept busy by friends.
Movies.
Restaurants.
And conversations.
About life and loss.
And God.

Dystonia is . . .

I end up being filmed by a local cable news channel.
Subject: nursing shortage.
I continue to write and develop new movement disorder material.
God certainly gave me a creative mind.
And dystonia.

I head off to Europe for several weeks.
Not realizing the adventure awaiting me there.

Dystonia is . . .

I arrive in Dusseldorf.
In ice and snow.
Rather unusual weather.
The train ride to Munster is about one hour.
Icicles cover tree branches.
Reminding me of what untouched beauty is.
Christmas wine greets me at the train station.
As I walk towards my aunt's apartment.
Already sipping on wine.
Neighbors recognize me.
And one only hears "Guten Tag".
After arriving at my aunt's apartment, I immediately head towards a
shoe store.
Seeking Hiking boots.
Snow covers the cobbled streets of downtown Munster.
I munch on plenty of German and Swiss chocolate.
Having temporarily forgotten about my dystonia.
Which hasn't been that bad.

Within days I send postcards and letters to those in the US.
Wishing them a good holiday season.
And a Happy New Year.
The talk in Europe is not of the impeachment proceedings but of
European Unification.
Banks carry the Euro.
Some is posted on walls for viewing.
Use for the general population is expected to be soon.
The year 2001.
My aunt and I begin planning for a quick escape.
Maybe Florence, Italy ?

The Swiss Alps ?
Vienna ?
A striking deal catches our attention.
7 days on the Turkish Riveria.
For 260 US dollars.
We decide on a Friday to go.
By Sunday we are there.
Via Istambul Airlines.

Dystonia is . . .

Turkey.
An ancient land.
With a rich heritage.
Deep poverty.
Varied landscape.
Gold.
Leather.
And Turkish carpets.

Blue plastic bags litter streets.
And highways.
A garbage collection disposal system failure.

Our hotel is classified as a 5 Star.
Plenty of Germans occupy the hotel.
Many wish to escape the post-holiday blues.

Each day we are fed well.
Buffet style.
Delicious Turkish food.
Salads of all types.
Tangerines and other fruits are plentiful.
As is Baklava.
And apple tea.

We take several tours into the interior of Turkey.
Avoiding the Kurdish area.
Disputes exists there.
An area not open for tourism.

The land is rugged.
As are the people.
Houses are built in three levels.
To house the entire family.
A level for each generation.
Poverty is clearly visible.
Goats and sheep graze along highways.
Tractors being used for transportation.

Our guide speaks excellent German.
Having obtained a degree in textile engineering from a German
University.
We walk among Roman temple ruins.
Climb Acropolis theaters.
Over 2000 years old.
Massive chalk-colored tombstones scatter the landscape.
Orange trees planted amongst them.

I am left wondering who lived in the temples ?
Who attended the theaters and dramatic plays ?
Who carved the remaining massive tombs ?
Who occupied the Roman and Greek baths ?
Who were the people who existed here ?
What were they like ?
As individuals ?
And as a society ?

Who am I ?
And what can I offer to society ?

An entire day is spent scrambling among these ruins.
Looking for historical signs of the past.
My hiking boots prove to be more useful.
Than when originally bought.
And I want to spend additional time among the ruins.
To think.

A gentleman in our tour group resembles an actor.
I call him the "Gregory Peck" of our group.
His companion practices Homeopathic medicine.
I find myself discussing dystonia with her.
In Turkey.

Dystonia is . . .

Fourth day in Turkey.
Strange lights light up the dark nighttime sky.
At dinner we learn of US missiles being fired upon Iraq.
Regardless we continue with our activities.
Including manicures.
And hair-cuts.
The Bazzar.
Aromatic spices fill the air.
Indian saffron.
Peppers.
People mingle.
And shout.
As one passes by their goods.
Trading and bargaining entrench the market.
Many Germans leave carrying leather bags.
Silk scarves.
Spices.
Calvin Klein T-shirts.

I leave Turkey having invested in a authentic hand-woven carpet.
Along with pictures and memories.

The New York Presbyterian Hospital awaits me.
My co-workers are glad to see me back.
I enjoy working with many of them.
All are highly-skilled.
I am impressed with The Open-Heart Unit.
I find myself working there frequently.
The level of nursing skill in this unit is commendable.
And I am in awe of many of them.
As they are with me and dystonia.
Which certainly surprises me.
Many want to learn more about the disease.
And me.
Why ?

Dystonia is . . .

A week has gone by.
The weather resembling my feelings.
Four week follow-up appointment with the dystonia expert.
The toxin has not worked at all.
We review treatment options.
The number of options are becoming increasingly limited.
I sit and listen.
Closing my eyes.
To prevent tears from forming.
I hear.
That I am not a candidate for this . . .
And this.
And this.
Frustration and fear begin building.
Brain surgery.
The only words I hear.

I'M MOVING TWO

My dystonia expert sits down.
Rubbing his eyes as he removes his glasses.
I see fatigue.
And disease frustration.
He does not know what to do with me.
All because of a phenomenon called "paradoxical inhibition".
That defines my dystonia.
A feature seen rarely in dystonia.
Inappropriate muscle activation and deactivation.
Integrated with complete muscle silence.
What am I supposed to do ?
I don't even know why I have this disease ?
I hear nothing else.
Except the words : brain surgery.
As I sit in silence.
In fear.
In anger.
These feelings are not addressed during the office visit.
I leave the office thinking.
And hoping that I do not end up crying.
As I head towards Bloomingdales.
For a free make-over.
Part of a contest.

Dystonia is . . .

What is this disease doing to me ?
Will it take me from my job ?
A job I love.
Critical Care Nursing.
What do I do ?
Give up ?
What do others with dystonia do when they reach this point ?
A time when treatment options have failed ?
And are limited.

I cannot recall what was said during the office visit.
I only heard the words "brain surgery".
To a degree I feel devastated.
And completely lost.
Overwhelmed.

I complete my shift within the Open Heart Unit.
Asking for an easy assignment.
Even though I'm on the verge of tears.
Every half hour.
But I keep myself together until I get home.

I begin investigating and asking about brain surgery.
From colleagues within the Neuro ICU.
Thinking and analyzing.

Botulinum toxin C is available in Italy.
Money is needed to make it available for patients here.
Half a million dollars.
So says my dystonia expert.

There are risks involved with surgery.
But then it may alleviate all the abnormal movements.
That would be a relief.
For me.

I finally call my aunt.
To inform her about the latest news.
I end being hysterical on the phone.
I do not want to worry my mother.
But within 24 hours my mother is on the phone with me.
Calming me.
And asking me "what is going on ?"
She will be present at my next appointment.
To question the dystonia expert.

I'M MOVING TWO

116

I finish a six day work week.
And sleep for two days.
Doing nothing.
But thinking how to raise 500,000 dollars.
For others.

My aunt calls.
To check up on me.
For this I am grateful.

I hate this disease.
Will it rob me from more dreams ?
From goals and desires ?

I feel angry that these issues are not a focus for many physicians.
What does a person do when they have a disease without a cure ?
What sort of care do these people then require ?
Are many of my counterparts in the same situation ?
What is optimal dystonia care ?

Redefining dystonia care.
A potential new goal for me.
How does one go about doing this ?
Without alienating others.

I begin reading books.
About fund-raising.
A difficult task.
Something I know very little about.

The Neuro ICU sustains me during this time.
D. always making me laugh.
As "Lordy, Lordy" echoes in the Unit.
On busy nights.

BEKA SERDANS, RN

Dystonia is . . .

It's been six weeks since that dreadful office visit.
I cannot erase the words "brain surgery" from my mind.
I feel restless.
And angry.
I begin finding myself awake at night.
Unable to sleep.
Because of two simple words.
When combined together.
Bring about images.
Images of brain tissue.

I continue to feel restless.
Despite working six 12 hour shifts in a row.
Nearly impossible for a healthy nurse to do.
I , on the other hand, do it.
Often.
May be too much according to my friends.
The Open Heart Unit has been busy.
A great deal of respect permeates the Unit.
Never have I met or seen such a group of dedicated colleagues.
Patients are on ventilators.
Tubes hang from bed side rails.
Bottles containing potent medicines are infused at high rates.
Intravenous bags glimmer in the dark.
Along with red lights that sparkle from other equipment.
Despite my own bad news I am able to give compassionate care.
I tend to forget my own problems.
When I'm in this Unit.
As patients are shipped in and out.
During each shift.

The staff begin to ask me questions about dystonia.
Initially some are afraid to ask.
But I am open to any questions.
Even the physicians begin asking.
During one shift I end up explaining the disease.
To a first year intern.
In front of a unresponsive patient.
Who is waiting for a liver transplant.
Our conversation lasts 40 minutes.
He, the physician, is now well informed.
About a disease I hate.

Dystonia is . . .

I hate this disease.
Its limitations.
And lack of optimal treatment.
Definitely, no cure in sight.
I continue to feel restless.
Sleepless.
Discouraged.
Disappointed.
And angry.

I call my mother.
Informing her that I'm coming home for 3 weeks.
One of my best friends is having surgery.
Another best friend is suffering from "care giver role fatigue".
With her father being admitted to an area hospital.

I have scoured the Internet for additional brain surgery information.
The procedure is called a pallidotomy.
And often is utilized to control Parkinson's disease symptoms.
But has also been used in dystonic patients.
With varying success rates.

The procedure involves ablating the area of activity of excessive neurotransmission in the brain that cause too much muscle contraction.
The more I read about the procedure.
The less inclined I am to undergo the procedure.
There are risks and benefits.
Will the abnormal movements stop ?

Unclear questions exist.
I confer with some of my nursing colleagues.

A resourceful colleague named E.
Questioning eyes as I relate some new up-to-date diabetes information.
Nurses have a history of "eating up their young".
She is a seasoned nurse.
With flamboyant scrub tops.
But an intimidating attitude presents itself at first.
At change of shift time.
I end up feeling as if I've done a horrible job with my patients.
I stand my ground.
And leave in a hurried fashion.
To only return in 12 hours.
Apparently E. spent part of the shift reading up on diabetes.
Something that comes naturally for me.
I am a Certified Diabetes Educator.
Which is to be renewed this year.

E. no longer intimidates me.
Despite her questioning eyes.
Soulful eyes mixed with compassion.
I respect her a great deal.
And I inform her of this.
To her surprise.
V. is just as warm and lovable.

Just about all who I meet at CPMC are.
Respect is reinforced in the speciality units.
From one to another.
Being "needed" is important to all.
A sense of belonging.
Much valued as I work alongside my colleagues.
A.M and S.F always ensuring that "I'm alright".
P. always working with a sense of coolness and calmness.
And dignity.
Along with an Angel.

Dystonia is . . .

Choice-less.
A nuisance.
Interfering with everything.
Like a two year old toddler who invades the kitchen cabinetry.
Unleashing anything and everything.
Despite parent reprimands.

I have been swinging on a pendulum.
Back and forth.
Some days are occupied with "lets do the surgery" thinking.
Other days turn into "lets avoid surgery" altogether.
I remain restless.
Not sure of what to do or not to do.
M.P. from the Neuro ICU listens easing some of my fears.
Do I simply live with the disease as it is ?
Or do I seek treatment ?
Those are my two choices.
I have to pick one.
Back to scouring the Internet.
Infoseek and Yahoo.

I arrive back home.
To be greeted by my mother and a big hug.

My mother sees my fatigue.
And senses my worries.
My sister from Boston arrives.
It is Easter Sunday.
A day of celebration.
I end up sleeping for two days.
Physically and emotionally exhausted.

My aunt questions "whether New York is killing me ?"
It's not.
Dystonia is.
To choose or not to choose treatment ?
Question of the century ?
Or question for a dystonic ?

Easter Sunday dinner.
My mother has gone overboard with cooking.
A natural talent for her.
She feeds me and my two sisters too well.
A new creation is set upon the table.
A layered cranberry jello cream mold.
Simply delicious.
We all devour it in a matter of minutes.
Realizing that we're not a pack of wolves.
But simply hungry.
For some homemade cooking.
Desert follows.
A scrumptious Rum cake.
Containing half a cup of Bacardi Rum.

Conversation centers on dystonia.
Somewhat unusual.

My sisters ask plenty of questions.
About my treatment options.

But at this point I'm simply tired.
Of a disease that reshapes itself.
And allows little control.

I want to rest.
To hide.
To feel free again.
From the effects of the disease.

It has carried an emotional toil.
We all have challenges and certain paths that we must cross.
Mine are certainly cut out for me.
But God only gives you as much as you can handle.
He must think that I can carry much.

I've taken a tour of my garden.
Tulip and daffodils are not yet blooming.
It will be a late blooming season this year.
I cannot wait to get out and start scavenging through my garden.
Where violets and yellows predominate.
My Alaskan daisies should thrive this year.
As should my Columbine.
Colorado's national flower.
It will feel good to feel the soil.
Earth.
Under the gentle Spring sun.
For now, the soil is too moist.
And rather muddy to a certain degree.

Garden.com.

Dystonia is . . .

I've worked in my old ICU.
New York stories are shared again.
And laughed about.
Chuckles arise within the Unit.
All are waiting for the Dateline segment.
Patience is of essence.
A virtue that not all have.

The last two days have been wonderful.
My friend survived her surgery.
Without any drastic hypoglycemic reactions.
I spent much time with her after surgery.
The two of us.
Simply sitting.
And reminiscing about the last ten years.
The length of our friendship.
Many ups and downs.
Joy.
Sadness.
Fear.
Tears.
Laughter.
And plenty of jokes
That only the two of us understand.
Much love exists between the two of us.
I regard her as my older sister.
She relates seeing me in a vision.
Before we met.
It was God speaking to her.
She had been asking Him for a "best" friend.
Well, she certainly got one.
Me.

I spend several hours working in my old ICU.
The pace is slow compared to New York.
Questions about Dateline never cease.
We must simply sit and wait.

There are new faces in the ICU.
In the entire hospital.
Where did they come from ?
Who are they ?
Did everyone leave as the "merge" began ?
Between two hospitals.
With two different employee cultures.

One night I spend in the local theater.
With M.J.
Seeing two movies.
For the price of one.
I'm sure we are not the only ones.
Sneaking from one show to another.
Both movies were unusual.
Not to my liking.
Little cinematography.
That captured little of the essence of each story.
Or my attention.
I continue to investigate my treatment options.
I feel more settled.
Less restless.
My garden needs a clean-up job.
Sunshine.
Spring wind.
A rake in hand.
I begin attacking my garden.
My garden will be over-run with daisies'.
One of my favorite flowers.

BEKA SERDANS, RN

I realize that I do not want a cure for dystonia.
Rather I want a treatment option that will maintain
  my current level of functioning.
I want to obtain a degree in journalism.
Work behind the scenes.
Of broadcast journalism.
The journalism bug has certainly hit me.
More so than I expected.

I want to do so much.
Before dystonia overruns me.
Doesn't everyone have goals ?
Dreams to be fulfilled ?
Of course, they do.
Some are ambitious and have the drive to do so.
Others simply dream.
And do nothing.
I'm ambitious.
I have the drive to do much.
I want to change the way dystonia is viewed.
By those who walk the streets in a straight line.
I spend ten hours in the ICU.
Once again it is busy.
Plenty of work to do.
Patient care needs to be met.
Families to meet.
To exchange words.
Or simply to comfort them.
Among a changing environment.

I've been working on my research paper.
About 20 pages in length.
My research boss is assisting me.
A couple more graphs to complete.
Then one final review.

By both of us.
Over dinner and a computer.

Dystonia is . . .

Kosovo.
A region of fear.
And despair.
Two ethnic groups cannot live together.
The pictures on TV are agonizing to watch.
Irregular lines of people.
The young.
The very old.
Who already have seen so much.
I see a 95 year old man.
Being wheeled in a wheelbarrel.
Unable to walk.
Hopeless eyes.
Not enough food.
For so many people.
As I watch the news reports.
I am reminded of the second world war.
And all the walking my own family did.
Walking from Latvia.
To American and British zones.
Escaping both the Germans and Russians.
Ruthless people.
In a ruthless situation.
The same now recurring in the Balkans.
Site of World War 1.

When are people going to simply stop ?
Simply be humane to one another.

Love one another ?

BEKA SERDANS, RN

Dystonia is . . .

The wind blows the leaves in the opposite direction.
Yet the sky is as blue as ever.
And I feel good.

I've located a neurosurgeon.
Who is willing to evaluate me.
A sense of relief.
For me.
And no one else.

Only I know my dystonia.
Its behavior.
Characteristics.
Features.
Only I know it's there.
No one else.
But me.

Time to head off to work.
Another shift.
Hopefully there will be time to eat dinner.

I have not seen A.
I hope to.
On the sixth floor.
Orthopedic land.
Embodied by casts and traction devices.
Pulleys and handbars.
In every room.

I end up working a 17 hour shift.
7 PM to 12 noon.

I'M MOVING TWO

128

Carrying the heaviest patient assignment.
And writing endlessly on one very ill patient.
I even draw diagrams.
To clarify surgical incisions.
I go home.
To only return in a matter of hours.
To work a 13 hour shift.
2 am to 3 PM.
The Unit is too busy.
Not enough staff.
I am grateful for the hours.
It implies Employment.
Functionality for me.

I was able to take care of my patients.
And did so , very well.
My mind is less occupied with the thoughts of "brain surgery".
I feel hopeful.
Not as helpless.
I meet several new staff members.
All are surprised that I also work in NYC.
Some find me fascinating.
I don't know why ?

I've consumed too much pizza.
Chicken wings.
And Pepsi.
We've been ordering out.
In the Unit.
Families watch us as we work and eat.
At the same time.
I admit a new patient.
With a mouthful of sugar cookies.
And jellybeans.

This week will be busy.
I've been sifting through photos.
To enlarge into prints.
For donation.
To an Auction.
Committed to raising money.
For dystonia research.
Chosen are four pictures.
Two from Turkey.
Focusing on the sea and stones.
Stones scatter the beaches of the Turkish Riveria.
Of all shapes and sizes.
Still-life photography.
Third picture from Salzburg, Austria.
My garden Cosmos being the last entry.

It will be interesting to see how much these photos fetch.
Good publicity for me.
A hidden talent.
Of mine.
That few know about.

God gives a person many gifts.
One simply has to find them.
And use them.
One never knows where God is leading you.
A question that so many try to answer.
Some succeed.
Others do not.

I am relieved to find myself back on track.
Less worried.
About the future.
And about dystonia.
I have much to say at my next appointment.

I'M MOVING TWO

Why must a patient feel guilt about their disease ?
Their symptoms ?
Should they ?
Patients must be able to validate their fears.
Acknowledge their guilt.
But they must never apologize for having such feelings.
The sun and moon cross paths.
As they do, do they apologize to one another ?
Obliterating one another's rays several times a year.
We must hold on to feelings.
Physicians are trained to help sort them out.
When we cannot do so.
Is this too much to ask ?
I don't think so.
Something to think about.
When I circle JFK in a two weeks.

It's been cold.
Garden work must wait.
Singing in the rain.
Singing the Brooklyn blues.
Similar to Manilow.

Snow covers the grass.
On April 11 1999.

Renewal.
Rejuvenation.
The beginning of a new work week.
My mother tells me to rest.
Instead I write.
Awaiting news from Columbia University.
School of Journalism.

Floodgates of distress.
Unbelief.
Impatience.
Disturbed.
Irritated.
Faithless.
Fearful.
Rebellious.
Floodgates of dystonia.
Is anyone out there listening ?
Does anyone want to ?

There should be someone out there.
To simply listen.

For the time being I feel better about myself.
And dystonia.
Although the pain involved remains.
To a lesser degree.

Crisis in Kosovo.
Air bombing campaigns continue.
Is anything being accomplished ?
People are still running.
Trying to escape.
Trying to live.
Among cities made from plastic.
Tents.
So much help is needed there.
I want to help in some way.
The crisis is expanding into other areas.

What is the mission of one man ?
Named Milosovijc ?

I'M MOVING TWO

Europe has been devastated by so many wars.
Racial hatred.
Ethnic cleansing.
Yet, America remains the "melting pot".
For so many.
What does the future hold ?
For Europe and America ?

Dystonia is . . .

It is a beautiful day.
Cool.
Brisk.
Clear blue skies.
But atrocities continue in Kosovo.
As I sit in my garden.
Not sure if I am working tonight.

Repeated updates can be seen and heard on MSNBC.
Regarding Yugoslavia.
What can be done ?
To help the innocent.
The old and the young.

Prayer.

Time to read some new diabetes info.
Food, exercise and insulin.
A dynamic combination.
A physical toil for many with this disease.

Dystonia is . . .

I receive a letter.
From my dystonia expert.

Confirming a negative antibody test result.
To toxin B.

A surprise.
That brings on emotional upheaval.
And questions.
Why ?
Why did the toxin not work ?
Are too many muscles involved ?
Is the dosing matchable to me ?
To MY dystonia ?

Sometimes I don't even understand my dystonia.
I know it's there.
And that's all I want to know.

I'm certainly in a jam now.
New decisions have to be made.
To rearrange appointments with other experts.
Or not ?

To receive the toxin or not ?
And risk antibody exposure ?

Confusion.
Indecision.

I climb into my car.
To simply drive.
Anywhere.
Within time I find myself in a bookstore.
Reading about decision-making.
In health-care.
And broadcast journalism.
How to become an author.

I'll have plenty of questions.
For the dystonia expert.
Hopefully time will be on my side.
And I can get answers.
On what to do ?
Or not do ?

Two basic questions.
Basic everyday questions.
Faced by many.

The other day I passed by the Chemotherapy department.
It's been six years since my father left me.
My mother.
Who still looks beautiful everyday.
He would come in every week.
Sit in a Lazy-Boy chair.
Be poked with needles.
And allow cancer-seeking drugs to do their job.
He would sit.
Quietly.
As my mother paced.
Outside the room.
I would run down from the Unit.
To ensure that all was O.K.

Are things ever O.K. with cancer ?
The same thought applies to dystonia.
And any other disease or situation.

I think guilt is eating at me.
I feel frustrated.
That my dystonia is so different from everyone else's.
Why ?
During office visits I can sense my dystonia expert's own frustration.

About my dystonia.
What can I do to make it easier ?
For him.
He desperately wants to make things better.
For me.
And for so many others.
But often I see fatigue in his eyes.
Yet, a persistent drive prevails.
So, often I simply sit there.
In the office where my dystonia poster hangs.
Letting my dystonia expert do the thinking.
Because I don't understand why I have this disease.
And because I don't want to think about the disease.
And deal with disease guilt.
Did I do something to bring this disease on ?
Did I work too much ?
Not sleep enough ?
Not eat the right foods ?
I admit.
I eat too many Haribo gummy bears.
My teeth will be falling out soon !
Do I have ineffective coping mechanisms ?
Is it because I did not enter medical school ?
But this is no longer a goal.
New goals have been formulated.
Did I not exercise enough ?
Has thyroid disease played a role in disease development ?

Guilt.
Guiltless.
Devoid of experience, mark, or sign.
Free of guilt.
This is what we all feel and want.
I think everyone feels this way.
At some point in time.

With this disease.
Especially the young.
ME.

Dystonia is . . .

I've returned to New York.
With my mother in tow.
Her second time in the big city.
The sun brightens the pavement.
As we pace the streets and avenues.
Eventually heading towards the dystonia expert's office.
A visit I'm hesitant to attend.
I think I'm simply tired.
Of a disease.

I get evaluated by a neurosurgeon.
Highly intelligent.
And gifted.
In the area of brain surgery.

Deep brain stimulation.
An option open.
Is it for me ?
Or someone else ?

I remain tired.
On an emotional level.
I donate my materials to the Auction.
With mixed emotions.

We arrive at the office.
And sit and wait.
For the dystonia expert.
To arrive.

BEKA SERDANS, RN

He meets my mother.
And is slaughtered with plenty of questions.
And anger.
Frustration.
Fear.
Indecisiveness.

Treatment options are reviewed.
Again.
And again. .

But many involve side-effects.
That could interfere with my job.
I'm not ready to give up on nursing.
I'm still good at it.
Without it I become a dystonic label.
Disabled.
And depressed.
I do not want to be forced from my job.
And its excitement.

Phenol.
An old surgical antiseptic.
When injected into muscle.
Destroying it.
A permanent feature.
Is this what I want ?

Maybe I don't even know what I want ?

Rest. .
Peace.

Dystonia is . . .

I've been invited to an author's reception.
At the Sixth International Dystonia Symposium.
To be held in British Columbia.
In a city called Victoria.
A city always in season.

Initially I accept the invitation.
But as the date nears.
I send a letter informing them.
The Dystonia Medical Research Foundation.
That I cannot come.

I am afraid.
To see so many others with various forms of the disease.
It only makes one question the issue of "disease progression".
And I'm simply afraid of this issue.
Because only I know my dystonia.
No one else knows.
But me.

Within days I receive a phone call from The Foundation.
Convincing me to come.
I call my mother to see if she would like to come with me.
Reply : no.
I think that she is afraid of the disease as well.
But from a different perspective.
A parent's perspective.

My younger "Bostonian" sister wants to come instead.
I admire her willingness and response.
That there is nothing to fear.

Flight arrangements are quickly made.
From New York to Vancouver to Victoria.
We find ourselves in Row 36.
The last row on the 757 Boeing aircraft.
Several feet away from the lavatory.
A system in overuse the entire flight.
We sift through all the Symposium highlights.
Looking forward to experiencing Victoria.
My sister listens to music and catnaps.
I fidget in my seat as I watch the film "Patch Adams".
Starring Robin Williams.
The main character of the film is a "soon-to-be" physician.
Who simply wants to help people.
Whether it is with humor, laughter or compassion.
A simple desire.
More physicians like this are needed today.
Many simply do not know how to relate to us.
To those dying.
To those seeking to live.
To those hunting for a cure.

I can relate stories of individuals with undiagnosed dystonia.
Whom have been referred to physicians.
Neurologists.
Psychiatrists.
Physiatrists.
Chiropractors.
Physical Therapists.
And more neurologists.

Is this appropriate care ?
And what is being taught to medical students ?
Are there any answers to this question ?

I'M MOVING TWO

Before I left for New York.
I literally ran into my own internist.
With training in Endocrinology as well.
We met by chance.
On the Fourth floor.
He simply asked me "how I was ?"
Giving undivided attention.
To me.
A human being.

Five hours pass.
We land in Vancouver.
Custom lines are long.
As we admire the airport.
Structurally built with steel and glass.
The sky being visible from all angles.

Anticipation and Eagerness.
Await us as we climb aboard a small aircraft.
Headed towards Victoria.
Images of dystonia begin to formulate in my mind.
My sister tells me to look at the sea and lush green islands.
Down below.
I do.

We are ten years apart.
But have sister- ties that are unbreakable.
During the entire flight she made sure that I was "OK".
This can be a burden for family members.
If one has a chronic disease.
Especially one that is as weird as mine.
I admire her.

But then she is my sister after all.
I am lucky more so now than when we fought over "Barbie dolls".
And whose clothing belonged to whom.

BEKA SERDANS, RN

Dystonia is . . .

Tears.
Crying.
From happiness.
That I have such a sister.
Along with one in Rochester.

Timberland.
Fir trees.
Greenery.
Unspoiled beauty.
Spectacular.
A photographer's delight.

Dystonia is . . .

Victoria.
A jewel set amidst God's beauty.
20 minutes from Vancouver.
A city situated on an island.
Surrounded by sea and foam.
An area of exploration.
Blooming flowers.
Window boxes.
Exotic petals.
Ambience.
Friendliness.
Seasoned with history.
This is Victoria.

My sister and I are ready to explore.
Our adventure begins.
Within the walls of The Empress Hotel.

I'M MOVING TWO

Site of The Sixth International Dystonia Symposium.
Waiting in line at the Reception counter.
I see many of my counterparts.
A mixture.
Of symptoms.

Some I can see are suffering.
Having difficulties walking.
Or simply standing straight.
But the hotel personnel do not seem bothered by these effects.
Either they were well informed about dystonia.
Or they all are compassionate people.
I commend them for displaying sincerity.
Towards us.
A special group of people.

Efficient check-in.
We admire our room.
Opening all the closet doors and chest drawers.
Cleanliness seeps through the ceiling and walls.
An iron board is quickly found.
As are the gym, sauna and swimming pool.

A short nap is taken.
I review the Symposium's schedule.
I think of D.C.
A co-worker.
Who lives four blocks south of me.
A native New Yorker.
Coming from a large family.
Of many girls.
Partially raised by her grandparents.
Just as I was.
Gregarious.
With a wealth of knowledge.

Twenty years of critical care nursing.
Who utilizes therapeutic touch.
A staunch believer in morals.
And God's words.
I liked her the minute I met her.
In the Open Heart Unit.
Her laughter is contagious.
Something needed in critical care nursing.
I admire and respect her a great deal.
As I do every staff member in this Unit.
I doubt that they all know how much I respect them.
Their knowledge base is as wide and open as the sea.
As are their hearts.
Off to the Welcome Reception and food.
Before I know it I find myself at the dessert table.
I choose two slices of Angel Food Cake.
Pouring on the thick berry sauce.

No choking spells.
Relief for me.
I found myself choking on food at work.
Several weeks ago.
That included Angel Food Cake.
I rarely eat at work.
Surviving on Pepsi during most of the shift.

How does one tell another person that you often eat in a flat
position ?
Vertical positions aggravate my dystonia.
Inducing further abnormal movements and tremors.
How does one eat then ?
Nothing until one reaches home.
And privacy.

What a ridiculous disease !

The room is crowded.
My sister finds us seats.
As Introductions are made.
Followed by applause.
A lengthy reception.
Many cannot sit still.
Postures and sensory tricks erupt throughout the room.
Collars, wheelchairs and braces are present.
I wonder if those without dystonia who are present.
Feel "out of place".

I want to say the following words :

These are our days.
They belong to us.
And every other person with dystonia.
Much will be shared.
Exchanged.
And learned.
Hopefully laughter and humor will prevail.
Compassion felt.
As the Symposium begins.

I meet a man.
Who shares his experiences with failing treatments.
I spend 45 minutes with him.
Educating him.
About where to go for treatment.
Who to contact.
I listen.
In the role.
Of patient advocate.
A role that I would like to emphasize to others.

BEKA SERDANS, RN

The man thanks me graciously.
Saying that it was worthwhile to come to the Symposium.
Because of ME.
I'm grateful for the complement.
We exchange addresses.
In a matter of minutes.

Jet-lag arrives.
Before we know it sleep drifts over both of us.
Yet morning arrives

I sit in on lectures.
Always observing others.
While my sister sits basking in the sauna room.

I hope my plants are still viable in my New York apartment.
I hear that it's been near 90 degrees.
Luckily they're all sitting in pots and pans.
Filled with water to the rim.

During the lectures I meet more people.
All seeking a listening "ear".

The afternoon is spent ambling through the streets of Victoria.
Shopping.
And spending money.
We try on jeans.
Skirts.
Anything that looks appealing.
My sister sifts through the clothes racks.
All done before The Author's Reception.

4 PM.
Start time for the Author's Reception.

I find myself in an elegant room.
And on a stage.
Over 200 people enter the room.
Finding their seats.
Sipping on tea in a matter of minutes.

I meet the other authors as well.
Readings begin.
I've never spoken in front of such a large crowd.
The last time I spoke in public.
Was in 9th grade.
English composition class.
Such a frightening experience.
That I ran out of the class.
Never to return to public speaking.
Until now.

I listen intently.
To all the readings.
And I admire everyone.
Who is willing to share their story.
And experiences.

My turn arrives.
I read my writing selections.
About disease labeling.
Dystonic.
Something none of us are.
We're people first.
Some of us being children.
Others adults.
But all intellectual.

Applause.
Applause.

The autographing and selling begins.
Many buy my book.
· I autograph all of them.
Shaking hands with each buyer.
And answering questions.
About anything concerning dystonia.
Being the last to leave.

I end up with writer's cramp three days later.
Eventually wearing a right wrist brace.
For several days at work.

· The evening ends.
At a Greek restaurant.
With a glass of red wine.
My sister and I celebrate.
The success of the Author's Reception.

The next day is filled with more lectures.
Focusing on the psycho social aspects of dystonia.
This is my focus.
Much more needs to be learned about this subject.
Within the context of the disorder.

Rental bikes available.
We decide to embark on a journey.
Along the sea coast.
My sister leading the way.
Acting as a "sensory trick" for me.
We bicycle for three hours.

Confirmation for me.
That the toxin is working.
We pass joggers.

I'M MOVING TWO

The sea.
Foam.
Beaches.
Grey stone.
Fascinating houses.
Wonderfully landscaped.
I try to memorize what I see.
To utilize in my own garden.

The sun shines.
A light breeze is present.
I simply cannot believe that I'm riding a bicycle.
Something I haven't done for awhile.
A simple activity.
For many.
It brings much joy.
To me.
A connection to my past.
A past free of dystonia.

Before we realize it.
It's time to pack.
And return back to Boston.
New York.
And sweltering heat.

Dystonia is . . .

Beka's back at Columbia.
In particular the Fourth floor.
Plenty of verbal Welcomes and hugs.
Plenty of work.
May be too much.
During spare time I write to many new people.
All met in Victoria.

The Author's Reception turned out to be a huge success.
Not a surprise.
But I'm still pleased.
And I tell everyone I meet about it.
Interest in dystonia increases.
Everywhere.

One day.
I'm going to be somebody.
Being somebody is important.
It gives one a sense of mission.
A sense of belonging.
We all need this.
In one way or another.

I work 5 twelve hour shifts in a row.
By the fifth day I need rest.
Two days off.
To write.
And write.
Something I do too much of.
Neck spasms are intensifying.
A sign of much needed rest.
But I still look straight.

Appointment day.
With the dystonia expert.
We cover the twister scales.
A set of study scales.
To evaluate the degree of twisting.
And posturing.
This time I find myself sitting straight.
I find myself laughing.
Because I'm straight.
My dystonia expert is pleased.
Success does wonders to one's self-esteem.

I'M MOVING TWO

He wants my brain.
A brain donor.
Me.
I simply chuckle.
But a brain donation program does exist.
And it's something to think about.
May be donation will further dystonia research ?
After one has left earth.
To enter God's world.

My office visit goes well.
Dominated by straightness.
I leave at 12 noon.
After working all night.
But not the least bit tired.
I finish some laundry.
And finish some writing.

A strike is being planned.
At my employment facility.
Mixed emotions.
Quality of care is at stake.
So are nurse-patient staffing ratios.
Regardless.
I do my work anyway.
So, I'm not sure what's at stake.
One can give quality care.
If one wishes to.
A simple deduction.
The new vocabulary of health-care.
Involves merges and down-sizing.
That's the reality of it.
The chief complaints involve the high staff-patient ratios per unit.
Especially nurses.

BEKA SERDANS, RN

Like me.
Papers are predicting a nursing shortage.
By the year 2001.
But it already exists.

I investigate the School of Journalism.
At Columbia.
To improve my writing skills.
A gift.
Given to a few.
By God.

Dystonia is . . .

I plan on receiving botulinum toxin B.
In September.
Before I testify in Washington, D.C.
In front of the Food and Drug Administration.
Something I've never done before.
But am willing to do so.
For the benefit of others.
No doubt that the toxin works.
Especially well.
But it needs to be made available.
To others.
Who failed other treatment options.
Who desperately need help.

Another idea comes to mind.
A guide called Dystonia Med Facts.
To help simplify medication use and knowledge.
Among us.
Correctly.
Written by myself.
From a patient's and nurse's perspective.

I'M MOVING TWO

Is this an advantage ?
Or not ?
I think it is.

I and my dystonia expert.
Decide to add a new drug to the treatment regimen.
Before the toxin completely wears off.
A drug from the U.K.
Some reading to do.
About a drug not available in the U.S.

I'm video-tapped again.
Proof of success.
Who killed the radio star ?
No one.
Except themselves.
Dystonia is not such a dreadful disease.
It's survivable.
Like anything else.
The power of prayer is the power of living.
This applies to dystonia as well.

I only have to work another three weeks.
Then back up to Western New York.
For a couple of weeks.
To bask in my garden.
And my beach.
Hopefully.
I'll tolerate the new drug.
Without any side-effects.
But my mother will keep an eye on me.
When do mothers not do so ?

BEKA SERDANS, RN

It seems that I may have an additional form of dystonia.
Myoclonic dystonia.
So, this is why my dystonia expert wants my brain !
Various forms of dystonia in one person.
Unusual.
When am I not unusual ?
A question I'm always asking God about.
He makes us all different.
Well, I'm different.
Just as the Harlem Globetrotters are.

Dystonia is . . .

Dystonia Med Facts.
A Beka Creation.

A man named Dr. Move.
A children's book.
To help explain movement disorders to children.
Another idea.
Another Beka Creation.

Dystonia is . . .

Back home.
One less resident of New York City.
The flight to Rochester takes over six hours.
Thunderstorms.
All along the East Coast.
Some of us frantically stand in check-in lines.
Hoping to rebook our flights.
Within hours I'm in the air.

Watching the city lights of New York grow dimmer.
Not to be seen for several weeks.

On my first day back I begin the new drug.
Only available in the U.K.
Home of scones and Lord's tea.
Drug name: Tetrabenazine.
I can find very little information on the Internet.
About this drug.
That can induce depression and Parkinson disease signs.
A risky drug.
To take for a few weeks.

Heat aggravates the drought in the area.
Many of my plants being barely visible.
Few flowering.
My lupines have disappeared.
A result of a local animal in the area.
Nowhere to be seen during the day.
Tan grass is visible everywhere.
Water rationing is in effect.
The lake levels being low.
This year.

We spend time at the beach-house.
Three levels exist.
Potted flowers abound.
The wooden deck extends into clear water.
But we all swim with water-sneakers on.
Due to dangerous mussel shells.
Non-edible.
But damaging to the feet.

Dystonia is . . .

My two sisters are present.
One taking a break from work in Boston.
The other being withdrawn.
Preoccupied with books and the sun.
Each day is spent in the water.
Walking along the Lake road.
Quiet time.
Just between me and my mother.
Simply talking about the future.
Oblivious of the sweltering heat.

My own thoughts return to my nursing colleagues.
In New York.
The workload.
I do miss all of them.
As I dive into the lake waters each morning.
Water temperature near 75 degrees.
Generating waves.

I write to several colleagues.
Including a letter of admiration to the staffs.
On the Fourth Floor.
And Director of Nursing.
A seasoned veteran in the field.
Aware of all of the nursing issues dominating health-care.
A person who calls me by my first name.
Some use my last name.
Which only makes me feel old.
I still consider myself young and vibrant.
Especially as my tan deepens.
To a golden brown color.
And lightens my hair.
Making me feel attractive.
Even in a bikini.

I'M MOVING TWO

SERD

Each night I fall asleep to the sound of waves.
Some nights are spent sitting on the dock.
Thinking.
Evaluating choices made.
Reading God's word.
Watching the stars.
Glimmer and shine.
Wondering whether this new drug will work.
I find myself writing to various magazines.
To get my story published.
To this date, no response.
And it is only August.
Vacation-time for many.

I re-enter my old ICU.
More fresh faces among the old.
Plenty of work to do.
Little time to exchange stories.
Over plenty of pizzas.
I sense and notice changes.
As I add some Recovery Room hours.
A degree of franticness exists on the floors.
Floors and staffs have consolidated their resources.
Yet there are too many patients.
And not enough nurses available.
Some of my shifts have been long.
Sixteen to Eighteen hours.
Double-backing of shifts.
Extra pay is provided to those of us who work extra.

In between patient care I write a speech and a poem.
Poem subject : Victoria.
Speech subject : Dystonia.

I'm invited to give my personal perspectives about the disease.
From a Genetics Company in Boston.
The speech goes well.
I learn more about genes.
12 for dystonia have been identified.
One for my type of dystonia.
Myoclonic dystonia.
A dystonia marked by unpredictable movements.
Jerk-like.
Lightening-like in appearance.
My speech goes well.
And I seem to impress all who are present.
Including the CEO of Sales and Marketing.
I see tears in his eyes.
I'm bombarded by plenty of questions over lunch.
Some are rather frank and direct.
But non-offensive in any way.

The future holds more speeches and travel.
An unexpected response.
Boston proves to be a success.
But under heavy construction.
Logan's airport is crowded with people and delays.
Fatigue prevails.
I arrive home late.
To watch imaginary situations on Television.

Thus far, I haven't noticed any problems with the new drug.
It works better in the evening.
My dystonia seems to worsen as the day progresses.
This is called paroxysmal dystonia.

I find myself thinking about the 12 genes for dystonia.
I must have one of them.
May be more ?

A choice is made.
Genetic testing to be done during my next office visit.
I hear that a vote for a strike.
At my NYC employment facility is imminent.
What lies ahead ?
For the staff ?
The facility ?
Nursing ?

I find plenty of hours within my old facility.
I begin writing my essays for the School of Journalism.
At Columbia University.
Ranked number one in the country for the study of journalism.

I continue swimming.
Beach combing.
Relaxing.
Between work hours.
That seem endless.
And marked by restlessness and franticness.
Is this the wave of future nursing ?
Bedside nursing ?
What lies ahead ?
For us all ?

I meet with friends.
Sometimes there doesn't seem enough time.
But they all remain within my heart.
Always.
Forever.
Signs of "forever friends".
Ties bound by the heart.
These are your best friends.
Those who'll come running at anytime.
Under any situation.

BEKA SERDANS, RN

To have such friends is to be lucky.
I consider them "gifts from God"
M.J.
L.
A.
And others.

I write to several of my colleagues in NYC.
I'm always writing.
This is what my mother says.
She learns how to perform manual traction.
On my neck.
To relieve the spasms.
The toxin has worn off.
Next toxin session due near Labor day.

I find myself getting plenty of rest.
Living near the water.
Nearly everyday.
I sift sand through my toes.
Watching it run through my fingers.
As I hear of the latest Kennedy news.
An American Tragedy.
But life gives and takes.
Life wasn't made to be easy.
The same circumstances run among the "have nots" and the "haves".
All have potential to better the world.
Yet violence, greed, money dominate the world.
Why must we think of these ideations during a tragedy ?
Each day should include a thought about the next person in line.
Whether it's in a homeless shelter, outside the ATM machine or in
a bookstore.
A lesson reinforced by tragic events.
Are we listening ?
Or thinking only of our own needs ?

I'M MOVING TWO

To compete against one another ?

Dystonia is . . .

Yikes.
Work has been busy.
I'm on call.
Reachable and available.
If needed, in the ICU.
I finish watching Nightline.
Turn out the lights.
Ready to drift off to sleep.
Within 30 minutes.
The phone shreaks.
It's the ICU.
They need me.

Need.
What is it ?
Something we all need or desire ?
Is it the same as "want".
Reflective questions.

I arrive in the ICU.
Looking like I just crawled out of bed.
I did.
I sip on Dr. Pepper.

To wake me up.
And before I know it.
I'm ready to work.
My one patient is 92 years old.
Named Alice.
Slowly dying.

A heart passively giving out.
She moans when turned.
I bathe her.
Talking to her.
About anything.
About love.
Her family.
Her life.
Her moans subside.
As I slowly rub her back.
And turn her on her right side.
Her favorite side.
She rests comfortably the rest of the night.
Her heart rate slowly dropping.
But still in the 50's by 7 am.

Healing power.
Something we all crave for.
On a daily basis.
Alice craves for peace.
I check on her all night.
Sometimes simply to caress her hair.
Giving her a sense of companionship.
As the dying process continues.
At its own pace.
A pace not defined by us.
But by God.

Another week in Western New York.
I wake up to a thunderstorm.
Pelting rain.
Much needed rain.

The grass brightens as the storm passes through the area.
Destroying flower petals.
But not my spirit.

Refreshingly cool.
And clean.
I run outside.
Barefoot.
Towards the mailbox.
Wet by the time I reach it.
Probably looking like a "wet rat".
My nursing magazines have arrived.
I'm in one of them !
I'm presented in a feature article.
"A Nurse's Battle with Dystonia".
Well-written.
A photograph appears.
It's me !
Who else I ask ?

I wonder about the title.
I've never considered dystonia a "battle".
Should I ?
I'm not at war with the disease.
I'm actually moving forward.
Planning genetic testing.
For my type of dystonia.
That has been tolerable.

I make copies of the article.
Mailing them to friends and colleagues.
I don't know what awaits me at Columbia.
Pride ?
Anger ?
Dismay ?
Disbelief ?
Wonder ?
I send copies to several dystonia-related organizations.

Surprise . . .
I'm an average human being.
Doing impossible feats.
According to others.

Sometimes I don't know what I'm doing.
I write to Newsweek.

The My Turn Editor.
Telling them my story.
With hopes of publication.

I send a copy of the feature article to my dystonia expert.
It'll be a surprise for him.
To a degree.
Finding a patient.
One of his patients.
Doing the impossible.
Conclusion.
God gave me dystonia.
For a reason.
Complete reason not quite understood yet.
By me.
I'm beginning to though.
Slowly.

I meet L.
At the hospital entrance-way.
I'm leaving.
She's arriving.
Finished another shift.
We stand and talk.
And talk.
And talk.
As hospital administrators arrive.

I'M MOVING TWO

In a rush.
We still talk.
Both of us being late.
For work and sleep.

Our conversations can be endless.
She's acted as my personal editor.
Reviewing much of my written work.
She's read an awful lot over the years.
Always acting as an advocate.
And the best of friends.

We both like the same Bible verse.
From Proverbs.

"A Friend loves at all times".

How true this is.
I'm lucky.
I've got several such friends.
Alleluia !
Am I lucky ?
Yes.
No doubts about that.

Next book.
Letters to L.
Letters to Best Friends.
Intriguing relationships.
Built by God and Love.
Available for anyone.
One simply needs to ask.
Who ?
God, of course !

Where do these ideas come from ?
God.
Who else ?

I'm on call again.

Dystonia is . . .

My neck has been pretty good.
But it has been deviating to the left.
The head sometimes being parallel with the shoulder.
Then I'm unable to walk straight at all.
Finding sensory tricks proves to be more difficult.
But the new drug seems to be controlling the myoclonic twitching.
This is better.
I'm due for the shots again.
In 18 days.
The countdown begins.
Again.
I call Columbia.
Telling them I'm on my way back.
My article has made waves.
Hopefully.
Good ones.

Dystonia is . . .

Headline News.
An earthquake has hit.
Struck.
An area I've visited.
Turkey.
Istambul.
The city where the East meets the West.
The beginnings of The Orient.

I'M MOVING TWO

Rubble.
Dirt.
Screams.
For help.
Escalate in the area.
I watch the news.
With intensity.
People need help.
I want to help.

Desperation.
Loss.
Grief.
My "battle" is meaningless.
Compared to the latest news.
It's time to take a look at the blue sky.
And what life really means ?
It can be gone in seconds.

Shaking ground.
Mud.
Vigilance.
From scientists.
Who watch the earth move and shake.

Screams.
Crying.
Tears.
Devastation.

Rescue needed.
And it arrives.

In the form of money, food and other aid.
A sign of people helping one another.
Instead of killing one another.

BEKA SERDANS, RN

September arrives.
Summer ends.
Yet, the sun still shines.
Brilliantly.

Time to head back to New York.
Streets.
Lights.
Excitement.
A place of constant kinetic energy.

I find my apartment in good shape.
All my plants have thrived.
Despite the intense heat.
Of the summer.
For a day.
I clean and organize.
Answer messages.
Making multiple phone-calls.
By day's end.
I find myself tired.
Physically fatigued.
Watching Nightline.

Dystonia is . . .

I arrive at work.
In pain.
Neck pain.
All ask "how I am "?
I find myself embraced.
By people.
Colleagues.
And a disease.

That remains.
Persists.
Refusing to go away.

The Units are busy.
Under constant activity.
I'm glad to be back.
This I tell to everyone.
But my thoughts return to a summer.
Spent in water.
And on the beaches of Lake Ontario.
Thinking about my mother.
And our many long verbal conversations.
About my father.
How they met.

Love at first sight.
Despite a seventeen year age difference.
My father was a "family man".
Always talking about his three girls at work.
Three girls.
With three different personalities.
One intense and highly intelligent.
Another with a sensitive soul.
Like him.
The third being energetic and carefree.
Easy-going.

My father.
Had brilliant blue eyes.
That knew everything about you.
Even if you were telling a lie.
A black lie.
A white lie.

A lie was a lie.
Honesty was a virtue.
Those crystal blue eyes I remember well.
Often I want to see them again.
Another look.
To see a loved one.
One more time.

My father.
Would take us sledding.
He would bring his skies with him.
And race us down icy hills.
Always letting us win.
Talented he was.
Committed and never faltering.
He was.
To us.
And my mother.

My mother still misses him.
Its been six years since he left us.
Sliding into a deep sleep.
After being ravaged by a disease.
Called cancer.

Why must people be ravaged by this disease ?
Why must there even be such a disease ?
Will there be a cure ?

My father.
Lived with the disease.
For three years.
Endless appointments.
Chemotherapy.
Radiation therapy.

Drugs.
Nausea.
Hair loss.
Fatigue.
Uncertainty.
Of the future.

Dystonia is . . .

Unpredictable.
Uncertain.
It never leaves.
I hate it.

I never know what to expect.
From this disorder.
What a disorder !
Complex.
And frightening.

I want to hide.
The self-image aspect of the disease.
Has hit again.
I don't want to be seen in public.
But, where does one hide in the big city ?
There's too much publicity here.
One learns to occupy oneself inside.
Away from everyone.
And the public.
Now I know.
One's dwelling makes a good hide-out.
From the public.
And from oneself.

BEKA SERDANS, RN

I write.
And write.
Putting words and thoughts.
My soul.
On paper.

Dystonia is . . .

A struggle.
It's been like that for the last four weeks.
I've had falls.
Total number.
Five.
Half of ten.
Worrisome.
Depressing.
On a sunny day.
I find myself.
Flat on a street.
In the middle of New York.
New Yorkers walk around me.
Silently.
Simply gawking.
I stare back.
As I stand up.
To curse at the sidewalk.
Quietly cursing at dystonia.
Is it the new drug ?
A side-effect.
Called Parkinsons.
Or is it my dystonia ?
Disease progression.

More falls occur.
I really begin to worry.

I feel down in the dumps.
Listless.
Helpless.
Not wanting to work.
Or be seen.
By the world.

I've had enough of running.
Within this hectic pace.
Thoughts begin to formulate.
It's time to head back home.
By the calm waters of the lake.
And the beach.
Where I can walk.
Me and my dog.

I've turned into a workaholic.
Is this a New Yorker ?
My allegiance is less with nursing.
Dystonia is winning again.
It's taking me from my career.
Ending it.
Forever.
Taking me from Columbia.
Where I've learned so much.
From amazing colleagues.
Skilled.
And highly devoted.

What do I do with the School of Journalism ?
I don't want to become a reporter.
Running around for the best story.
I'm a story by itself.
I can write.
Without a degree in Journalism.

BEKA SERDANS, RN

I'm tired.
Of running.
Non-stop.
Stepping off the train.
Walking down the streets.

I need peace.
Quietness.
As I struggle with falls.

I find myself in my dystonia expert's office.
Silent.
Crying inside.
Far removed.
From his questions.
I don't have much to say.
As I sway down the hallway.
Waiting for him to realign me.
Straighten the head.
Twist the neck.
In the opposite direction.
Push the shoulders downward.
Towards the floor.
It works for less than five minutes.
I want to cry.
Dystonia is taking me.
Away from New York.
And everything it has to offer.
Away from Journalism.
Away from my career.
Away from dreams.
Fulfillment.

I want to fight.
But don't have much strength.
To do so.
Successfully.
I've already fought since 1991.
When symptoms began.
A lifetime.
Away.

My dystonia expert senses this.
There's compassion.
And patience.
Acceptance.
And recognition.
At what the disorder does to a person.
The person.
This time.
Being Me.

Exhaustion.
My body craves for sleep.
A deep sleep.
One that is restful.
Instead I find myself up at night.
Walking.
Practicing.
Watching TV.
With the remote control.
Fitful sleep.
I watch old movies.
Starring Bette Davis.
Jimmy Stewart.
Montgomery Cliff.
Possessed by demons.
Fame.

Money.
Fortunes.
And eventually age.
And disease.

The remote finds itself switched on and off.
Throughout the night.
12 Mn.
3 am.
6 am.

As I practice.
Walking.
Straight.
Unsuccessfully.
With and without shoes on.
As the rest of the building sleeps.

Medication changes are planned.
I listen.
Not saying much.
As Columbus Day nears.
With parade expectations.

An internal struggle.
I don't want to give up.
My lifestyle.
My career.
It's too soon.
It wasn't supposed to happen yet.

Fear.
Of failure.
Of loss.
Return of the grieving process.

I'M MOVING TWO

I hate dystonia.
A short and simple sentence.
But it says it all.

I hate dystonia.
And what lies ahead.
Disability.
Disablement.
Defined by the CDC.
Social Security Benefits.

I'm tired.
Of dystonia care.
Repeated office visits.
I want out.

My lease ends in March.
Six months away.
What do I do ?
Leave.
Head to Europe for awhile.
To the Swiss Alps.
Mountain hikes.

Dystonia is . . .

I call my mother.
Telling her about everything.
The last four weeks.
She cries and worries for me.
I call my friends.
One by one.
All are ready to help me.
Is this what I'm fearing ?
Loss of independence ?
The arrival of dependence ?

BEKA SERDANS, RN

Do others worry about these things ?
Whether dystonia exists or not ?

The weeks go by.
I find myself on national TV.
Dateline.
Drug companies start calling me.
Asking how I accomplished getting on Dateline ?
The news magazine.
I have no answer for them.
Even if I did, I wouldn't tell them anyway.
People tend to use other people's ideas.
To benefit themselves.
Reaping rewards
For themselves.
Without thinking who provided the ideas.
A lesson I have learned.
Not an easy lesson to learn.
So, I no longer give my answers away to others.
For free.
Why should I ?
I'm the one facing career loss.
Disappointment.
And dystonia.
Isn't that enough ?

I do my laundry.
Permanent press.
Only.

Dystonia is . . .

The fall leaves begin to cover the sidewalks.
Of the Big City.

And I remain in turmoil.
Struggling with indeciveness.
Reality.
I'm due to take the writing test.
But I can't type 35 words per minute.
I schedule myself for the test anyway.
Journalism continues to intrigue me.

Is it the school ?
Name ?
Columbia ?
Status ?
Potential opportunities ?
For writing.

I attend a Dystonia Symposium.
In Richmond.
The South.
Colonialism.
And history overwhelms the senses.
I and a friend.
Drive 500 miles.
Into the Blue Ridge Mountains.
Colors of Fall ignite the senses.
Yellow and orange hues.
Glitter among sun rays.
A simple view.
Snapped by a photographer.
Three roles of film are used in minutes.
As images of Fall sneak by the back roads of Virginia.

We stop by a roadside antique shop.
Not knowing a thing about antiques.
As we sift through dust and old relics.
The owners.

A young couple.
Friendly and warm.
No questions asked.
But we're given a warning.
To avoid U- turns !

We spend two days roaming.
The hills of Virginia.
We arrive in Monticello.
Stopping at the Gift Shop.
First.
Before it closes.
I leave with postcards.
And a book.

"The Family Letters of Thomas Jefferson".
An intriguing man.
With questionable but honorable motives.
To be agreed or disagreed upon.
Once the book is read.

For some reason.
I've always been interested in American colonialism.
We find plenty of it in Williamsburg.
An ancient town.
Entrenched with modern equities.
Plenty of shops.
Too many.
But we go on a buying spree.
Me, focusing on books.
About early America.
Such a young country.
Compared to Latvia.
Whose capital, Riga, is over 1,100 years old.
Touched by Swedes, Germans and Russians.

I'M MOVING TWO

180

Just about everyone.

By the afternoon we take a break.
Sitting outside Baskin-Robbins.
That beckons us.
I enjoy a strawberry iced delight.
Smothered with Marshmallow sauce.
A. chooses a chocolate creation.
Topped with peanuts.
We watch passerbys.
Both trying to calculate.
How much money we've spent.
And the Symposium hasn't even started yet.

I end up crating Birkenstocks.
And books.
To our rented car.
We started off with six miles.
On the odometer.
Number now revealed : 548 miles.

We continue driving.
Back to the hotel.
A curvaceous two-lane highway.
That seems endless.
We both await to see the Headless Horseman of Sleepy Hollow.
We drive and drive.
A hunter appears out of no where.
But we continue on our way.
Exchanging our separate buying spree prices.

Basketville.
Spend two hours there.
Baskets hang from the ceiling.
They're everywhere.

And cheap.
Christmas gift ideas come to mind.
Along with the credit card.

The Symposium begins.
I meet new and old friends.
My Dateline segment is aired.
And applauded.
I'm met with gracious thank-you's.
For a job well done.
Some organizations haven't said "boo" to me.
Since the airing of the segment.
But I had no help in getting the story on dystonia out.
I did it all by myself.
No help.
But lots of work.

I meet one of the surgeons.
Involved with surgical denervation.
I may be a candidate.
Time to seek HMO coverage again.
Decision-making again.

My speech goes well.
Too well.
A long question and answer session.
The needs of people with dystonia are immense.
All carry similar stories.
Of mis-diagnosis.
Some struggle with canes and walkers.
I find myself to be the youngest one with dystonia.
At the Symposium.

I spend one evening.
In the whirlpool.

I'M MOVING TWO

Warm effervescent water encircles me.
I don't want to climb out.
Total relaxation.

A few hours are spent in a pottery factory.
Endless rows of pottery exist.
Filled with dishware and other items.
We leave with a few more items.

We spend the evenings driving.
Using up gas.
Eating at The Olive Garden.
Wendy's.
Friendly's.
Looking for historical statues.
And the cobbled streets of Richmond.

We leave the city.
Packed with plenty of stuff.
Little room.
To spare.

A. returns to Rochester.
I return to Columbia.
And another office visit with the dystonia expert.
I find a portion of this manuscript bound.
In a chapbook.
On amazon.com
Plenty of e-mails are answered.
I have a good visit with my dystonia expert.
No new drugs started.
The last one did a number on me.

I write up two brochures.
One on dystonia.

The other on Parkinson's disease.
I work five 12 hour shifts in one week.
I take a few days off.
Writing an article on the drug , Baclofen.
Used to control spasticity.

Dystonia. is . . .

Reminds you of what you had.
What you want.
And what you don't.

Indecision continues.
Surgery.
Stop employment as a nurse.

What is nursing ?
What has it become ?
As drills and hammers create new suites.
For new but old services.
I sense burn-out among staff members.
Not a good sign.
Fatigue and sick-calls rise.
Leaving units short-staffed.
Hoarding of supplies begins.
Linen shortages develop.
Over time.
But are now more visible.
Tempers are strained.
Voices strangled.
Of those questioning the merge.
Are we still professional ?
Or are we an expensive commodity ?
Are there any answers ?
Departments become rude to one another.

I'M MOVING TWO

184

Interaction.
Marked by rudeness.
Are we serving the same mission ?
That of quality health-care ?
We arrive fatigued.
To find heavy burdensome assignments.
I'm floated to several areas during the week.
The nurses express their frustration.
In the form of questions.
But I don't hear any answers.
Will we ?
What have we become ?
Nurses ?

Do I still want to be a nurse ?
What looms ahead for us as a group ?
Silence greets us only.

I slowly reach a decision.
Time to head back home.
Concentrate.
On prospective surgery.
That involves approval.
From my HMO.
Possible denial of care.
I begin developing a strategy.
To obtain treatment.
Possible success.

I choose not to go to Journalism School.
At least not in New York.
I think.
A writing degree.
May be more worthwhile.
The talent for writing already exists.

BEKA SERDANS, RN

Its been there all along.
Ready for cultivation.

Another plane falls from the sky.
Suddenly.
Unexpectedly.
Over 200 people on board.
Their flight path.
Is a routine one.
Along the Eastern Atlantic coast.
Bordered by greyness.

And plenty of rocks.
I think.
Of the passengers on board.
Most were settling themselves.
Into a long flight.
Sifting through magazines.
And anticipation.
That goes along with a journey.
A trip.
A holiday.
A home.
Vacation for some.

Silence.
Disappearance.
From the sky.
From international radar.

Slabs of metal.
With a pair of shoes.
A teddy bear.
Are found floating among the foam.

I'M MOVING TWO

The sea.
Can hide much.
Deep and hidden.
The wreckage remains.
Powerful.
Stirring.
Riveting.
Yet calming.
Such is the sea.
A creation.
With many stories.
Hidden from us.

Each day.
Questions arise.
Over the disappearance.
Of a plane.
And so many.

Who had dreams.
To only be swallowed up by the sea.

I hope I don't see the wreckage.
From the sky.
When I head towards Europe.
A continent to be bombarded.
By tourists.
As we near the Millennium.
45 days remain until the New Year.

I hear that Rome will be busy celebrating.
So-called "a jubilee celebration".
Is expected to consume the city.
Over the next year.

BEKA SERDANS, RN

Dystonia is . . .

Be still.
Be near.
Be far.

These phrases echo in my mind.
What do they mean ?
Life has been difficult the last few months.
The toxin worked only four weeks.
Twisting and turning returned in no time.
I warn everyone.
Including my colleagues.
That my symptoms will be worse.
Over time.
I feel tired.
Exhausted.
My neck and shoulders freeze up for 3 days.
Leaving me bedridden.
As the sun's rays filter through the windows.
Temperatures begin to climb.
As I become more frustrated.
At what ?
Dystonia ?

Dystonia care ?
I skip 2 of my appointments.
With my dystonia expert.
I don't want to receive any care.
What use is there ?
Symptoms continue.
I'm not heard.
I want to scream.

I call Florida.
To find out more about the surgery.
That can resolve symptoms.
Several dystonics call asking for help.
I can't offer them much right now.
I need help.
I feel listless.
As I gaze into the silver mirror.

I begin to sleep more.
Work less.
Not wanting to be seen.
Or heard.

$40,000.00.
Cost of surgery.
Another worry.
A call from my dystonia expert's office.
Where am I ?
Still here.
But frustrated.
I end up screaming at them.
Not knowing what else to do.
The simplest thing to do.

My neighbor jingles his keys.
Each day.
At 9 am.
The start of every work day.

Who's going to win ?
Me or dystonia ?

It's all a game.
A gambling one.

BEKA SERDANS, RN

With unknown chances.
I'm simply beat.
And don't have the energy to fight.
Fight what ?
A disease?
Or myself ?

I spend half a day at my dystonia expert's office.
Sleeping.
Waiting.
Sitting.
Pacing.
Another exam is done.
I scream.
About the pit.
I've been in.
A black one.
I'm now at the rim of the pit.
Hoping to not fall back in.

Expressed.
Anger.
Depression.
Helplessness.
Hopelessness.
Defeat.
Frustration.
Feelings felt by so many.
On a daily basis.
Many are able to climb out of the pit.
Others cannot.

I'm listened to.
Finally some relief.
By the time I've finished.

I'M MOVING TWO

I'm spent and listless.
Like a dog lacking water on a hot August day.
The toxin is reinjected.
Under my direction.
I show my expert which muscles should be injected.
Within an hour I'm feeling much better.
And can walk up Madison Avenue.
Without an intoxicated gait.
Twisting and posturing ceases.
People look at me.
I return their looks.
Smiling.

The battle is over.
I'm ready to fight.
1.5 million dollars is needed to create patient services.
Support for others.
A new mission.
Planted by my dystonia expert.
I thought I was a failure.
That he was going to give up.
On me.
And the rest of us.
Was I wrong !
Commitment persists.

Surgery is discussed.
To be done only in Florida.
By the most experienced neurosurgeon.
Procedure called "selective denervation".
Nerves to dystonic muscles are cut.
Alleviating symptoms permanently.

Only.
The disease itself persists.

I begin reading about fund-raising again.
I explain the latest details.
To all my colleagues at CPMC.
They listen intently.
With admiration.

I walk home one day with D.C.
And ask her quite frankly about this admiration.
And respect that my colleagues exhibit towards me.
Admiration is not to be questioned.
But simply accepted.
So she says.
We discuss many other things.
I encourage her to consider N.P. School.
She is warm.
Direct.
Loving.
Compassionate.

I make plans.
And return e-mails.
Refocused.
And redirected.
With an ambitious goal.

1.5 million dollars.
Where do I begin ?

Care 4 Dystonia.
Is formulated.
I begin to research non-for-profit organizations.
Calling some to obtain information.
About start-up costs.
A website is developed.

And reviewed.
An organization.
With a mission.
To create support services for people with dystonia.
I choose my Board of Directors.

All of whom accept.
Eagerly.
Wanting to help.
Establish the First Center of Excellence for Dystonia.
What a goal !
Accomplishable ?
Yes.
I begin sitting in local law libraries.
Reading up on legal issues.
And tax exemption.
A foreign language.
For someone in the area of medicine.

Be still.
Be near.
Be far.

I tell my mother about this new venture.
The phone is quiet.
Stillness.
Another form of silence.
Then I hear babbling.
Filled with excitement and support.
I hang up.
Not quite understanding my mother's excitement.

A logo is created.
Vision recreated.
As I wait for tax forms to appear in my mailbox.

BEKA SERDANS, RN

M.J. arrives for another visit.
To escape.
We walk the streets of NYC.
She admiring the architecture.
We talk endlessly.
She proofreads the web site.
Rain arrives.
In torrential downpours.
Soaking our clothes in minutes.
A pool of water stains my apartment floor.
Dryer use goes in effect immediately.
My neighbors listen to the noise we're making.
The building is relatively quiet otherwise.

That was then.
But this is now.
We reminisce about old times.
Nursing school.
Carribean adventures.
Filled with too many rum punches and sun.
Aggravated by sunburn.
And overloaded suitcases.

Wednesday.
I meet with my endocrinologist.
Who always listens patiently.
To all I have to say.
Weight down by seven pounds.
Have to eat more.
But how does one eat with a twisted neck ?
This I ask.
Otherwise, I'm in good shape.
In mind, body and soul.

I'M MOVING TWO

We run off to the new attraction in town.
Hennes & Mauritz, a Swedish clothing store.
Not unfamiliar to me.
Men join women in shopping for items.
. Dressing rooms are lined with people.
All shapes and sizes.
Hoping to find that special one item.
People carry loads of clothing.
Taken from half-empty racks.
I ask myself.
Haven't they seen a store like this ?
Nothing new to me as a European.
One of the most popular stores.
Across the blue Atlantic.
Where the Titanic lies.
Slowly corroding beneath the waves.
M.J. is easily overwhelmed.
By traffic, people, tourists and rudeness.
But she likes the dogs being walked along the streets.
Some behaved, others stubborn.
We do take out Chinese food.
Also chewing on Matza crackers.
Late into the night.
Trying to finish our conversations.

Dystonia is . . .

Surgery.
Planned for Fall.
Requiring approval from my HMO.
Help.
The law books come out.
Specifically contract information.
Help.
I call my dystonia expert.

Help is on the way.
Temporary relief.
Last dystonia treatment option.

I e-mail The Department of Neurosurgery.
At Columbia.
Offering them an unusual proposal.
R. helps me identify with the right people in the Department.

Heat and humidity.
One can barely sleep.
Air conditioners go into effect.
I receive bad news.
Another R.
With dystonia.
Has died suddenly.
Shock.
We were planning.
Promotion for Care 4 Dystonia the other day.
In a week's time.
I begin to miss him.
And his e-mails.
Advice.
Editing.
Knowledge.
And sense of humor.
Life gives.
And it takes.
It took R.
From me and so many others.
I end up working 70 hours in one week.
Trying to figure out tax-exemption forms.
During spare time.

SERD

I make an appointment.
For surgical evaluation.
In Florida.
Towing several neurosurgeons with me.
In an effort, to increase the number of neurosurgeons.
Capable of performing the procedure.
Last resort procedure for dystonia.
Selective denervation.

I hear expected dreadful news.
My wonderful mentor has died.
At a time.
When he was still needed by so many.
In particular, his wife.
Children.
Grandchildren.
I read his obituitary.
And cry.
As I have lost another important individual.
In my life.
Who taught me about compassion and medicine.
And the interactions of these two entities.
Cherished memories come to thought.
Hours spent in the Operating Room.
X-ray interpretation.
Chest tube use.
Pain control.
Laughter.
Professionalism
Dignity.
Conviction.
Dreams..
He fought a disease.
That did not eascape.
But lingered.

Heartfelt memories of him intercede my mind.
And dystonia.
A disease that seemed to fascinate him.
And the person behind it all.
Me.

Surgical evaluation looms ahead.
No fear yet.
Simply.
Nervousness of the unexpected.

To be continued.

If you'd like to contribute to Care 4 Dystonia,Inc. write to :
R.Serdans, RN
Care 4 Dystonia
440 East 78 Th Street
New York, NY 10021
http://www.care4dystonia.org/

GRAY-JACKET 5.5 X 8.5

Printed in the United States
6485

9 780738 828442